Elizabeth Wilhide

Converted

How to extend your home **up**, **down** and **out**

Collins

First published in 2007 by
Collins, an imprint of
HarperCollins*Publishers*
77–85 Fulham Palace Road
Hammersmith
London W6 8JB

The Collins website address is www.collins.co.uk

Collins is a registered trademark of HarperCollins Publishers Ltd

013   012   011   10   09   08   07
7   6   5   4   3   2   1

Editor: Zia Mattocks
Picture Researcher: Liz Boyd
Designer: Richard Marston

A catalogue record for this book is available from the British Library

ISBN 978-0-00-722940-2

Collins uses papers that are natural, renewable and recyclable products made from wood grown in sustainable forests. The manufacturing processes conform to the environmental regulations of the country of origin.

Colour reproduction by Colourscan, Singapore
Printed and bound by Printing Express, Hong Kong

Contents

Contents

Introduction

Don't move, improve! That is the message going out to today's homeowners, as they struggle to reconcile the changes life throws their way with a home that may fall short of accommodating their needs – or possessions – in a number of ways.

In Britain we spend a staggering £40 billion on home improvements every year, projects that range from basic repairs and maintenance to more complex conversions and extensions. Increasingly, it is money well spent. When house prices are in a state of flux and the costs of moving are rising, it can make good financial sense to spend the money that would otherwise have gone on stamp duty, agents' fees and conveyancing, as well as the actual removal itself, on improving your home so it provides a better fit.

Short of building a home from scratch, converting redundant areas such as attics and basements, rethinking the layout or extending outwards or upwards offers the best opportunity to shape your home to suit the way you want to live. Turning an attic into a home office, a cellar into additional living space or a garage into a teen annexe can help keep you in step with your changing needs and those of your family.

We ask a lot of our homes these days. On the one hand, they are our private retreats from the hustle and bustle of the outside world – places in which to unwind, recharge our batteries and express our personal tastes. But as more and more people choose to work from home some or all of the time, they can also be called upon to provide an efficient environment in which to earn a living. Then there are the competing needs of different household members and all the various activities and interests they bring

PREVIOUS PAGE
A sliding glass door and glazed partition open up a stairwell, making the most of available natural light. White décor also helps to spread the light around.

LEFT
A new kitchen is a popular form of home improvement and adds value to your property. This conversion has been planned to make a better connection with the garden at the rear.

to the mix. Sometimes it seems that our homes don't merely need to be flexible, they have to virtually shape-shift in order to keep everyone happy.

'Home improvement' used to conjure up a sort of low-level tinkering around the edges of things – new tiles in the bathroom, shelves built into an alcove, a fresh coat of paint – jobs that might be tackled with a little DIY expertise and a few spare weekends. Nowadays it is more likely to suggest radical change that requires at least some degree of professional help.

For most people, their home is the biggest investment they will ever make. Major conversion projects also cost money – quite substantial sums in some cases. For that reason it is important to make sure that whatever you are planning to do to your home will give you some payback in the future in terms of enhanced sale value or desirability. Putting in a new kitchen will have an immediate impact on potential buyers; conversely, substituting double-glazed units for original sash windows may knock value off your property at a stroke. It is also important that any work is carried out to the highest possible standard, in terms of both design and construction.

There is no getting around the fact that a substantial proportion of the housing stock in the UK dates back a hundred years or more. Rows of terraced and semidetached houses, whether Victorian, Edwardian or even earlier in period, have undeniable character and give many of our cities and towns a sense of continuity and rootedness in the past. What these houses may not provide, however, is the type of internal planning and spatial quality that many of us prefer these days. The same, on the other hand, is often true of much newer homes, which are typically designed along fairly conservative lines, in terms of both arrangement and detailing.

Fortunately, most houses are eminently convertible in line with contemporary expectations. Our desire for light, spacious, free-flowing living areas can be accommodated by extensions, changes to internal planning and new glazed openings that bring the outdoors in. You may be able to gain an extra room by converting your attic – or an extra level by digging down under your house. A whole range of clever spatial solutions can also be employed to keep your possessions in order and to support hardworking areas of the home such as kitchens and bathrooms. Even the humble garden shed can be pressed into service as a self-contained home office or guest room.

The popularity of home improvements and conversions can be gauged by the fact that such projects account for about half of the average borough's planning caseload. Moves are afoot to streamline the process of gaining planning permission and speed up the system, which should provide a further impetus to development. Not all conversion projects require permission, but of those that do, nearly 90 per cent eventually gain approval. This means that while official permissions undoubtedly represent a hurdle, your plans are unlikely to fall at it, as long as you have done your homework properly.

Converted provides the practical information, ideas and inspiration you need to make the most of the space at your disposal. As well as an introductory section covering the basic practical points – from budgeting to legal issues and employing others to scheduling – separate chapters cover different types of conversion in more detail, while individual case studies show a variety of different schemes in practice.

There's always room for improvement.

A substantial part of the process of any conversion takes place before the first contractor sets foot in your home. If the back bedroom needs redecorating, you can afford to act more or less on impulse – choose the paint and off you go. But alterations to your home that entail building work are a different story. Such involved projects require careful planning and assessment right from the start. When things go wrong, it is often because people have not done their homework, investigated all the options or foreseen likely areas of difficulty. The advice given in the following section applies to most types of conversion.

1 Groundwork

Assessing your needs

You have made one critical decision, which is to improve or convert your existing home to meet your current needs. Now it's time to nail down exactly what you're hoping to achieve. The first step is to assess what you already have, so you can establish how and where your home falls short of your requirements. Then it is a question of exploring the potential for change and drawing up a list of priorities.

ASSESSMENT CHECKLIST

- **It might sound like an obvious question, but what do you like about your home?**
  What has persuaded you to improve or convert it rather than move elsewhere? It might be the location – nice neighbours, local amenities, good schools, an easy commute – or it might be aspects of your home itself – architectural detail, good natural light, spatial character. Bear the positives in mind when going on to think about improvements. At the very least, you don't want to compromise any assets you already have; ideally, your aim should be to enhance them.

- **Does your home function efficiently?**
  Has it kept pace with your changing needs and requirements? Can you perform everyday tasks and routines without unnecessary effort? Think about routes around your home and the way practical areas such as the kitchen and bathroom are planned. Are there bottlenecks or areas that are difficult to access? Does basic servicing – water and drainage, electricity and other lines of supply – require upgrading?

- **Are you short of space?**
  Many, if not most, conversions are carried out for the principal purpose of increasing floor area. Think about where you are feeling the pinch most. Do you need another bedroom? A bigger kitchen? Another bathroom? Extending your home or converting a redundant attic or basement into a habitable space generally has a knock-on effect on internal layout. Changing the assigned functions of different areas in your home can often serve to make an addition or conversion more successful.

- **Spatial limitations may also arise when possessions accumulate. Do you have enough storage space or are you disappearing under mounds of clutter?**
  Incorporating additional built-in storage facilities within a conversion can ease the pressure on space. Conversely, if you are planning to convert an attic or basement that is currently used as a deep-storage area, will you be able to accommodate those possessions elsewhere?

- **What do you like to do that your present home prevents you from enjoying to the full or simply does not accommodate?**
  You may wish to make a career change and work from home, in which case you will need a dedicated work area. Or it may be that you haven't enough room to entertain or to put up overnight guests.

If you have a garden, is it easy to access from indoors? Does it serve as an extension of the living space?

Conversions and extensions can vastly improve the relationship between interior and exterior spaces, and even, in the case of attic conversions, provide the opportunity to create new outdoor areas such as roof gardens and terraces.

Think about existing spatial character.

Are the rooms cramped or awkwardly proportioned? Would you prefer an open-plan layout? The conditions of natural light are a key factor in our experience of space. Are present areas well lit? Would new internal or external openings improve matters?

Is the fabric of your home – both decorative and structural – in good condition, or are there areas that need repair?

Bracketing such work with a conversion project makes good financial sense, with the added advantage that you need to have the builders in only once. Changes to lighting and electrical infrastructure – for example, installing fixed lights or upgrading wiring – are often disruptive, so it makes sense to carry out such improvements at the same time as any conversion or extension. Similarly, if you are converting an attic, it often makes sense to renew the roof covering, guttering and flashings at the same time, if these are showing signs of wear.

Building work, particularly conversions that affect the external appearance of your home, has to conform to certain official regulations.

Are your proposals likely to win approval or meet local codes? If not, could you achieve the same quality and degree of space another way? Protracted battles with planning authorities or building inspectors will slow down your scheme and cause you unnecessary stress.

How long do you expect to remain in your home?

Try to imagine yourself in five years' time. What changes of lifestyle can you envisage? Will the improvements you are planning to make to your home serve you equally well in the future? Will they add to the resale value of your home?

DESIGN BRIEF

When it comes to improving, adapting and converting your home, there is sometimes more than one route to a desired result. The best solution may not be the most obvious or what first springs to mind, even if what you require seems to be very straightforward. Design professionals (see pages 28–30), who are experienced at solving spatial problems, can be very useful in this respect and may come up with a scheme that delivers improvements you had not even conceived of.

Before you take things further, draw up a wish list for change and think about where your priorities lie. This will help to clarify your thinking and can form the basis of a brief if you do decide to consult a design professional. Your budget may not stretch to everything on the list, but you should not be tempted to cut corners by postponing any essential repairs that will affect the long-term structural integrity of your home. There is no point spending a considerable sum of money on an extension if that means you cannot afford to tackle a serious case of subsidence.

A wish list represents what you would like in an ideal world, but don't despair if you need to compromise. Compromise can bring unforeseen benefits. One of the most viable sites for an extension, for example, is at ground level to the rear of a property, which naturally requires the sacrifice of some garden space. However, rear extensions, if properly planned, can improve the connection between indoors and outdoors so that home and garden truly flow into each other. At the same time, the groundwork required for the foundations offers the opportunity to relandscape the garden, introducing changes of level that deliver additional interest.

At this stage, you should also think about the quality of space that you prefer. Do you want to integrate different areas in your home in an open-plan layout? Do you prefer fitted or unfitted spaces? If you are considering adding on an extension, would you like something bold and contemporary or do you want to replicate the existing style of your house? These broad considerations will have a bearing on the type of solution that is best for you.

There are two basic types of conversion work: those that involve structural changes and those that do not. Structural changes are generally more expensive (though not always), more disruptive and subject to a greater degree of scrutiny from official bodies.

In many cases, distinguishing between work that is structural and work that is not is fairly straightforward. You may well need advice, however, when it comes to alterations to internal walls. Some internal walls provide an essential supporting or bracing role within the overall structure. If you remove a substantial part of a structural wall, you will need to introduce a compensatory element such as a steel beam to take the load. Other internal walls are merely partitions that serve to divide space rather than help to hold up the building. Partition walls are generally less robustly constructed, typically of studwork; they may sound hollow when tapped. If you are in any doubt, err on the safe side and consult a professional such as a surveyor, architect or structural engineer.

Nonstructural alterations and improvements include:

- Cosmetic changes, such as decoration, new surfaces and finishes, and simple fitting out.
- Putting in new kitchens and bathrooms or moving the location of existing kitchens and bathrooms.
- Moving or altering partition walls and replanning internal layout.
- Lengthening an existing window.
- Changes to servicing.

Structural alterations include:

- Making changes to load-bearing internal and external walls, including creating new external openings.
- Widening either existing openings or windows in external walls.
- Changes to roof structure.
- Attic and basement conversions.
- Creating new extensions.

A glazed roof sends natural light spilling down into a ground-level extension. Specialist advice is necessary for such structural work.

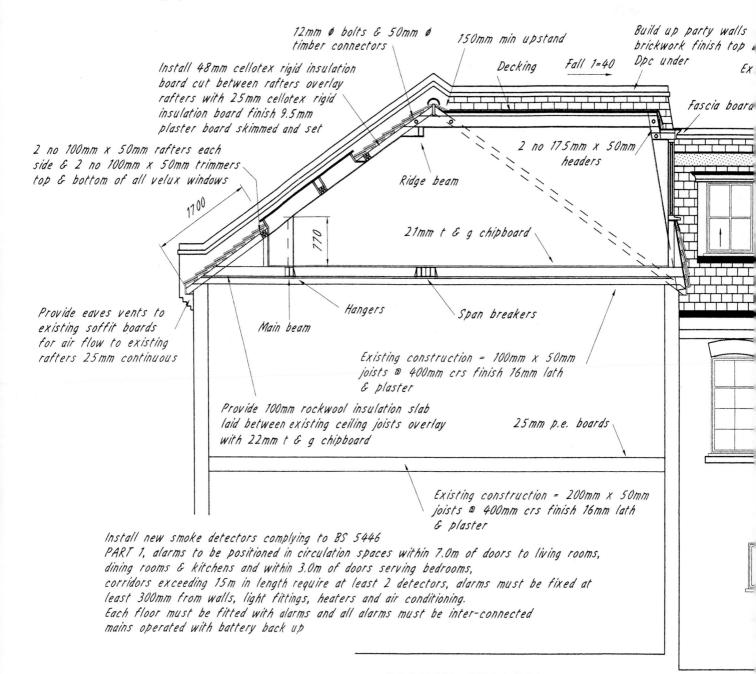

12mm ∅ bolts & 50mm ∅ timber connectors

150mm min upstand

Build up party walls brickwork finish top Dpc under

Ex

Install 48mm cellotex rigid insulation board cut between rafters overlay rafters with 25mm cellotex rigid insulation board finish 9.5mm plaster board skimmed and set

Decking

Fall 1=40

Fascia board

2 no 100mm x 50mm rafters each side & 2 no 100mm x 50mm trimmers top & bottom of all velux windows

1700

2 no 175mm x 50mm headers

Ridge beam

770

21mm t & g chipboard

Provide eaves vents to existing soffit boards for air flow to existing rafters 25mm continuous

Hangers

Main beam

Span breakers

Existing construction = 100mm x 50mm joists @ 400mm crs finish 16mm lath & plaster

Provide 100mm rockwool insulation slab laid between existing ceiling joists overlay with 22mm t & g chipboard

25mm p.e. boards

Existing construction = 200mm x 50mm joists @ 400mm crs finish 16mm lath & plaster

Install new smoke detectors complying to BS 5446 PART 1, alarms to be positioned in circulation spaces within 7.0m of doors to living rooms, dining rooms & kitchens and within 3.0m of doors serving bedrooms, corridors exceeding 15m in length require at least 2 detectors, alarms must be fixed at least 300mm from walls, light fittings, heaters and air conditioning. Each floor must be fitted with alarms and all alarms must be inter-connected mains operated with battery back up

SECTION THROUGH

Full architectural service (see page 29) includes the preparation of detailed drawings of the proposed works, which can form the basis of negotiations with planners as well as a blueprint for construction and specification.

atching
e with

to 1000mm
indow

Clad dormers in 9.5mm sheathing
plywood to prevent racking forces

Double up rafters at
dormer cheeks

Flashing

Code 4 lead skirt

Ornamental fascia

Provide ridge tile vents
= to a 5mm continuous
strip

Flashing

Soakers

REAR ELEVATION

21

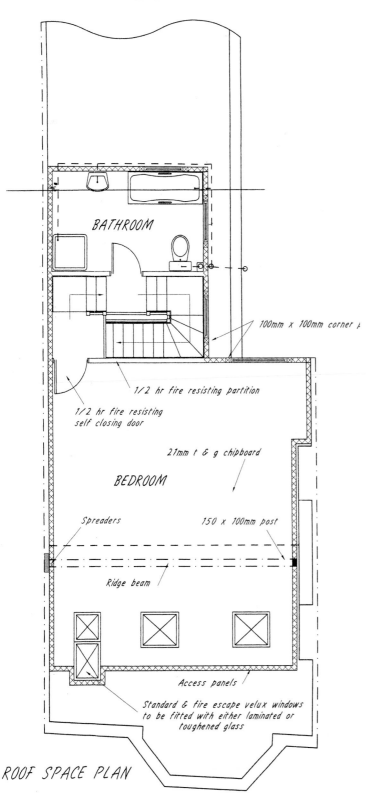

BATHROOM

100mm x 100mm corner ⌐

1/2 hr fire resisting partition

1/2 hr fire resisting
self closing door

27mm t & g chipboard

BEDROOM

Spreaders

150 x 100mm post

Ridge beam

Access panels

Standard & fire escape velux windows
to be fitted with either laminated or
toughened glass

ROOF SPACE PLAN

MAKING A PLAN

A scale plan is a useful aid in the process of deciding which changes you would like to make to your home. Once you have put the spatial relationships on paper, it is easier to visualize improvements. If you are intending to change only one particular area, such as a kitchen, you don't necessarily have to include the rest of your home, but it can be useful to draw a complete floor, especially when you are considering factors such as access.

A scale plan, or even a sketch, can be a useful way of opening a dialogue with a design professional, even though he or she will produce their own drawings in due course. The same is true if you are buying a fitted kitchen or bathroom, for instance, and taking advantage of in-store design services, or explaining your wishes to a contractor.

A scale plan showing the alterations to a roof space to convert it into an additional bedroom and bathroom.

- **Begin by measuring the area(s) in question.** Choose one system of measurement – either metric or imperial – and stick to it. In Britain and the EU metric is the norm for materials, fitted modules and appliances. Use a steel measuring tape and be as accurate as you can – you may need someone to help you. Break an irregular area down into discrete geometric shapes.

- **Transfer the measurements onto a rough sketch plan.**

- **Mark the position of fittings and features on the sketch** – the position of windows and doors, alcoves, chimney breasts, light switches and power sockets, built-in cupboards, radiators, appliances, fixtures and other details.

- **Make a scale plan using graph paper.** Choose an appropriate scale. Working at 1:50 – where 2cm (¾in) equals 1m (3ft 3in), or one square equals 50cm (20in) – is adequate for assessing general spatial relationships. If you are replanning a kitchen or bathroom, however, 1:20 will give you more detail.

- **Because appliances, fitted units and bathroom fixtures come in standardized modules, you can use the scale plan to plot their optimum arrangement.** Working to the same scale, draw the shapes of units or fixtures, cut them out and move them around on the plan until you find the optimum workable layout.

- **Use the scale plan to investigate different layout options.** Could a door be moved? Would you improve access or save space if it opened the other way? Are existing servicing arrangements – plumbing, heating or electrical infrastructure – inhibiting you from making the best use of the space?

Groundwork Assessing your needs

Budgeting

Early on in the planning process, you should set a budget in place. A budget isn't just a financial limit – though it is a crucial parameter – it is also a means by which you can achieve the best value for money.

Few of us can draw on unlimited funds or are indifferent about how much we spend on home improvements. Working out a detailed budget keeps plans realistic from the beginning and helps to avoid the type of overspend that tends to result when you proceed with only a vague notion about how much things cost. At the same time, it is also possible to spend too little on a conversion or to allocate your funds in ways that are not cost-effective. Budgeting allows you to re-examine your project and determine where money would be best spent so you achieve the optimum result.

Are you spending too much?
Spending too much on a conversion is not simply a case of spending more than you can really afford and getting into serious debt as a consequence. You could also be spending too much if the conversion does not add significantly to the value of your home. You may wish to consult local estate agents to gain an idea as to whether what you are planning will enhance the resale value of your home or not. If you intend to stay in your home for the foreseeable future and house prices are predicted to rise, such considerations are not so critical.

Are you spending too little?
Have you allocated enough funds to complete the work to a satisfactory standard? It is a false economy to compromise on basic quality of workmanship. If you are currently planning to put in a new kitchen, but other areas of your home need improvement, it can often be more time- and cost-effective to bracket the work, rather than spread the improvements over a number of years. Labour and material costs tend to go up year by year.

Are you eligible for a grant?
Various government agencies provide grants for some types of conversion. If your home is listed or is of exceptional historic or architectural interest, you may be able to apply for a grant to cover the cost of necessary improvements or maintenance. Financial help may also be available for improvements that increase your home's energy efficiency – such as installing solar panels or wind turbines on your roof.

A substantial part of the cost of any conversion work is taken up by materials – not only bricks, mortar and roofing tiles, but also flooring, worktops and other internal surfaces. You may have your heart set on a stone floor for your new kitchen extension, but if that means there is less in your budget for other essential elements, you may wish to opt instead for a material that delivers the same degree of practicality for a lower price. Similarly, state-of-the-art fixtures and fittings can devour a disproportionate amount of your budget, money that might be better spent in different ways to enhance the sense of space. Custom-made elements also cost more than standard fixtures that can be obtained off the shelf. Only you know where your priorities truly lie: budgeting will bring these into sharp focus.

Another variable is your input into the project. If you are a practical, hands-on sort of person, you may feel perfectly relaxed about tackling some of the work yourself – if not the heavy construction, then perhaps internal finishes, decoration and tile-laying. Only you know your capabilities, but do not be tempted to do-it-yourself solely as a means of cutting costs. If you are inexperienced, you run the risk of making a poor job of it, losing money through wastage of materials and even endangering your physical wellbeing.

Depending on the nature of the project, you may be able to save money by coordinating the work yourself, hiring each tradesperson directly rather than relying on a main contractor. Similarly, you may also wish to take on the task of sourcing materials and fittings. This role requires a good head for organization rather than brute strength or specialist skills. You must also have a good grasp of what needs to happen and in what order (see Sequence of work, pages 38-9) and be prepared to devote enough of your time to ensure that things run smoothly. This tends to mean you will need to be on site most of the time to take deliveries and deal with problems as they arise.

COSTING YOUR PROJECT

Work out the figures in as much detail as you can right from the start. If you are employing a builder or contractor to carry out the work on your behalf, ask for a detailed estimate so you can assess how your money will be spent and identify possible ways of economizing. No two projects are the same, but here are some broad areas to consider:

- **Demolition and disposal costs** – you may need an area cleared or an existing extension torn down to make way for new work.

- **Hire costs of any specialist equipment,** such as mini-diggers or scaffolding.

- **Cost of the building work itself,** both labouring and specialist contracts.

- **Interior surfaces and finishes** – for example, flooring and tiling.

- **Fittings and fixtures,** including details such as switches and door handles.

- **Custom elements**, such as high-performance glazing.

- **Fees of consultants** – designers, architects, surveyors, structural engineers and other specialists.

- **Planning application and legal fees,** if required.

- **Costs arising from disruption** – for instance, nights spent in a hotel or meals eaten out if building work makes your home unliveable for a period of time.

- **Loss of income.** If you plan to tackle some of the work yourself, how will that affect your earning capacity over the period of the project?

- **Cost of financing the project** – for example, interest owing on bank loans.

- **Contingency.** Add at least 10 per cent of the total cost of the work to your budget as a contingency fund in case things go wrong. This margin represents your financial safety net and will help you to deal with any unexpected hitches that arise.

Special features, such as these strengthened-glass panels used on an upper walkway, are often more expensive than standard elements, particularly if they have to be custom-designed.

Most conversions, with the exception of those that are very straightforward, are generally too expensive to be financed directly out of your earnings. This leaves you with a number of different options for raising the money:

- **Cash in hand.** Savings, investments or a lump sum that you might have inherited.

- **Bank loan.** Many banks provide bank loans specifically for home improvements. If you already have an existing mortgage with your bank and you can demonstrate that what you are planning will increase the market value of your home, you may find the bank will look favourably on your application, provided it is satisfied that you can afford the repayments.

- **Remortgaging.** Cheaper than a bank loan is to remortgage your home to cover the costs of conversion. Because the additional borrowing is spread over a long period, you will pay lower interest. Naturally, this option will apply only if you have sufficient equity in the first place.

- **Credit.** The most expensive way of financing home improvements is through credit. Many stores offer some kind of financing scheme to help you to spread the costs of a new kitchen or bathroom, for example. Like the terms offered by credit-card companies, the interest on such loans tends to be high.

Groundwork Budgeting

Employing others

Statistics tell us that DIY is no longer as popular as it once was. Perhaps we have more competing demands on our leisure time these days, or perhaps we are more prepared to pay for a professional result. Whatever the case, if you are planning to convert your home in any significant way, you are definitely going to need to employ others to carry out a substantial proportion of the work.

Arguably, nothing will make a greater difference to the success of a home-improvement project than finding and hiring the right people for the job in the first place. This is one area where it really pays to do your homework and put in the time researching the options.

WHO DOES WHAT

Professions and trades involved in design and building are very diverse. The first step is to acquaint yourself with what they do. Depending on the nature of your project, you may need some or all of the following help:

- **Planning and design advice.** Architects, designers and in-store design services can help you to come up with a viable scheme (in terms of planning and legal requirements), as well as one that meets your brief and is within your budget. Some firms specialize, for instance, in kitchen design or loft conversions.

- **Technical advice.** You may need to consult a surveyor or structural engineer to determine ground conditions for any work that involves laying down new foundations, to sort out boundary issues or changes to party walls, or to calculate the size of new structural members, such as beams. If you suspect that there may be defects in your property that are likely to affect its structural stability, you may wish to commission a thorough survey.

- **Basic building work.** The nuts and bolts of construction generally include demolition, brickwork and blockwork, timber framing and the installation of services. Larger building firms or contractors may be able to cover all the necessary trades; more usually, plumbers, electricians and carpenters are employed on a subcontract basis.

- **Specialist building work and suppliers.** Roofing and erecting scaffolding tend to be specialist jobs that are subcontracted out by builders.

- **Specialist fitters.** Installing nonstandard materials, such as stone flooring or high-performance glazing, are usually jobs for specialist fitters.

- **Specification, sourcing and supervision.** Keeping the lines of supply in place, ordering materials and fixtures so that they arrive on site at the right time and supervising the standard of building work are all roles that can be usefully handled by an architect or main contractor.

WHICH ROUTE TO CHOOSE?

There are a number of options open to you when it comes to getting the work done. At one extreme, you might wish to opt for a full architectural service, which, once the design has been agreed, will limit your involvement to signing your name at the bottom of cheques. At the other extreme, if you are confident and capable, and the project is straightforward, you may well be able to manage quite a bit of it yourself, with the assistance of a number of subcontractors as and when they are needed. In between are other approaches, each with their own merits.

FULL ARCHITECTURAL SERVICE

For a fee, generally calculated as a percentage of the overall building costs (about 10 per cent in Britain), you can expect the following:

- Thorough consultation to come up with a detailed brief that meets your requirements and your budget.
- Advice on planning issues and building codes.
- Liaison with any specialist consultants, such as surveyors or structural engineers.
- The development of a scheme, from outline proposals to detailed drawings suitable for submission to the planning department.
- Negotiation with planners and other authorities to ensure that the scheme wins the necessary approvals.
- The drawing up of a full specification (materials and finishes) and the preparation of working drawings.
- Selection of contractor, usually by sending the scheme out to tender to a shortlist of candidates with whose work the architect may already be familiar.
- Preparation of contract documentation with contractor.
- Supervision of the works when they get under way, including necessary inspections.

- A final inspection to note any defects and have these put right, known as 'snagging'.

Full architectural service, in other words, is a one-stop shop. Employing an architect is, of course, no guarantee that things will not go wrong, but it does mean that you have a professional advocate looking after your interests and dealing with the planners, builders, subcontractors, suppliers, service engineers and so on, on your behalf. While on paper it may seem the most expensive option, employing an architect may actually save you money in the long run, or at least get you more for your available budget. The one proviso is that you have to be absolutely clear from the outset about how much you can spend.

PARTIAL ARCHITECTURAL SERVICE

A good choice, especially for those who don't have a clear idea of what they want or how to realize it in design terms, is to opt for a partial service and commission an architect to come up with a scheme that meets your needs and budget, and subsequently see the proposals through the planning process, if required. Flat fees can often be negotiated for such work. While getting the work done will then be the responsibility of your builder or subcontractors, you will have got past the major legal and planning hurdles and will have a scheme that is structurally feasible. If you wish to take it a stage further, you could have your architect prepare working drawings for the builder.

PACKAGE DEALS

Companies that specialize in a particular type of conversion or extension are increasingly common. Within this category are loft and basement conversion firms, as well as suppliers of conservatories and fitted kitchens and bathrooms. Most will tackle the necessary work from design stage to completion, although this is not necessarily the route to take if you are after a bespoke result or if you are planning changes to your home across the board.

MAIN CONTRACTORS

Most complex conversion projects will require the services of a main contractor – in other words, a builder or building firm. Main contractors usually have few people on their books on a permanent basis; instead, they supplement core staff with specialist subcontractors when they are needed. The advantage of employing a main contractor to construct your project is that you have someone on site to organize the work, order materials, hire plant, deal with the subcontracts and generally keep everything running smoothly. In addition, there is the protection of the contract itself, which gives you a means of redress if things go wrong (see Contracts and agreements, page 35).

Employing a main contractor generally costs more than hiring the necessary tradespeople directly yourself. If your project is straightforward and does not present many organizational challenges, you may not need to choose this option.

SUBCONTRACTORS

Many of the tradespeople we employ on a casual basis fall into this category, including plumbers, carpenters, electricians and decorators. Few conversion projects will proceed to completion without the services of at least one or two subcontractors. They tend not to be all-rounders, so don't expect your electrician to be able to plumb in a sink or your carpenter to install some new lighting. Simple projects can be run directly on a subcontract basis, but you have to be prepared to take on an organizational role, which may mean ordering supplies, coordinating deliveries, hiring equipment and scheduling the work so that everything happens in the right order. At the same time, contractual arrangements are not as formal, and you will find you have less redress if something goes wrong.

FINDING HELP

Scare stories in the press and television programmes that chart disastrous home makeovers in excruciating detail have given many people a deep suspicion of all building professionals. It is important to overcome these misconceptions at the outset: extreme cases may make good copy or push up the viewing figures, but they are far from representative of the profession at large. In reality, few architects are deaf to reason or insistent on imposing an alien aesthetic on their hapless clients;

equally, few reputable builders do a disappearing act as soon as the roof comes off, or spend all their time on site drinking tea.

The first step, therefore, is to approach the task of employing others in a positive light. There is a good reason for this. If you expect the worst, you will inevitably be less discerning when it comes to weighing the merits of different firms or individuals and so more likely to have a bad experience in the end. There are many competent professionals out there – it is merely a question of tracking them down. What you are looking for is evidence of skill and competence, such as the right professional accreditations, sufficient experience in the type of work you want done and good references.

Competence is the bottom line. What is also important is finding professionals who are on the same wavelength as you. In design terms, this may mean an architect or designer with a portfolio of work that appeals to you or that displays the type of spatial qualities you would like to achieve in your own home. In other respects, it means 'someone you could do business with' – a person you feel comfortable with, whom you trust and with whom you can communicate easily. Employing people to work on your home is more like entering into a professional relationship than making a simple commercial transaction.

- **Begin the process early.** The better professionals tend to get booked up, so plan well ahead.

- **Professional bodies, institutes and trade organizations** generally publish lists of members, which may help you to locate someone in your area with the right qualifications and training. Many of these bodies offer a complaints procedure that may give you some redress if things go wrong.

- **Local newspapers and trade magazines** also carry listings of design and building firms.

- **The Internet** can be a good way of going shopping for a design professional. Many architects and designers have websites illustrated with completed projects. Surfing the Net can cut out a great deal of the legwork involved in finding a designer whose work you like.

- **Word of mouth** is one of the most popular ways of finding a professional. Ask friends and neighbours for recommendations, especially if they have commissioned the same type of work. Bear in mind any differences of expectation when evaluating their opinion. For instance, if your friend is a stickler for detail and highly organized, he or she may be less than satisfied with a builder who, while competent, had a more laid-back approach. That should not necessarily rule out that builder from your shortlist, especially if you tend to take a relaxed approach.

Groundwork Employing others

A bedroom in a converted loft has its own integral bathroom, separated by a half-width partition. Both parts of the space are lit by rooflights set into the plane of the roof.

If you are planning to engage an architect or building firm, rather than a series of subcontractors, the next stage is to narrow down your list of candidates to a shortlist of three. Provide each company with a list of what you require, in as much detail as possible, and ask for an itemized estimate of what the work will cost, how long it will take and when it could be scheduled. At the same time, ask each firm for three references and take them up.

The more specific you can be about your requirements – even down to detailing such as 'brushed-steel socket covers' or 'lino flooring in the bathroom' – the more readily you will be able to make informed comparisons once the estimates come in. Be wary of those estimates that come in the form of a vague ballpark figure and those that are suspiciously low. We all like to get value for money, but an estimate that is much lower than the others should set alarm bells ringing – a good, experienced professional who wants the work won't be doing it for next to nothing. High estimates can indicate a rip-off merchant or cowboy outfit, but more often they reflect the fact that your project is too small to be profitable for the firm.

If you need to compromise, scheduling is where to do it. You may be tempted to pick the firm that can start right away, but if that means paying more or going with a firm that otherwise wouldn't be your first choice, think again. Unless there is a compelling reason why you can't afford to wait a little – for example, it's usually inadvisable to expose your home to the elements during the winter if you can help it – it is better to be patient and postpone the project until your first choice is available.

- **Don't give yourself an unnecessary deadline if you can avoid doing so.** Wait until Christmas is over, for example, rather than give yourself extra stress hoping that the works will be finished in time for the holidays. Around Christmas many suppliers become overstretched in any case, which can cause delay to your programme. If you really need to convert your home before the new baby arrives, start well in advance of the delivery date.

- **Avoid scheduling noisy or disruptive works during periods when family members need peace and quiet** – exam time, for instance.

- **If extensive outdoor work is not required, you may save money by having the work done out of season when there isn't so much demand.**

Depending on whom you are hiring, you will need either to draw up a contract or to obtain a letter of agreement. Architects and main contractors work on a contract basis; subcontractors are hired less formally, usually by letter of agreement. Don't be tempted to settle the deal on a nod and a handshake, or imagine that insisting on paperwork will make it appear that you lack trust. Reputable professionals will want to see terms put down in writing, for their sake as much as yours.

If you are employing an architect, he or she will prepare the formal contract with the builder on your behalf. Another option is to use a solicitor. Standard short contracts, written in simple terms, are in common use in the building trade and are perfectly adequate for most conversion projects.

A contract should include:

- **The services, materials and work** you can expect for your money.

- **An agreed schedule** of how long the work will take.

- **The payment arrangements.** Payments are generally made in stages, as various aspects of the work are completed. This gives the builder an incentive to stick with the job.

- **The percentage of payment to be retained for defects** – 5 per cent is standard.

- **An agreed procedure to follow should things go wrong.** One of the most common ways of incurring extra cost or running over schedule arises when plans or specifications are changed once the contract is signed. The contract ought to set out what should happen in this case. Sometimes such variations are unavoidable – your builder may uncover a structural defect, for example, or the material you have specified may turn out to be unavailable. On the other hand, many clients change their minds countless times once they start to see things taking shape around them. Such 'extras' or variations to the contract can be very expensive and disruptive. All variations should be put in writing to prevent future disputes.

A letter of agreement is a simpler document and, although it is legally binding, you will have less redress if things go wrong. It should set out, on the subcontractor's headed paper, a quotation and schedule, and whether or not materials and fixtures are included. You may wish to pay a subcontractor a small sum upfront to cover the costs of materials, but it is advisable to reserve the remainder until the work is done. Similarly, agreeing a day rate is often a bad idea – you might find the work stretches on indefinitely.

MANAGING THE WORK

Even if you do not intend to manage the work directly yourself by coordinating work on site, sourcing materials and organizing deliveries, you still have a role to play in the project's successful completion. The following common-sense guidelines should help you to survive the works with your nerves intact and still on speaking terms with your builder:

- **Maintain a courteous working relationship with those you employ.** If you have followed the steps above, you should have confidence in your choice. Trust and respect on both sides goes a long way to achieving a good result.

- **Allow access to basic kitchen and toilet facilities.** It's not necessary to spend all day relaying countless cups of tea to the plasterer, the chippy and the chippy's mate, but a little hospitality does not go amiss.

- **Before the building works start, remove all valuable or breakable items from the area in question.** Electronic equipment can be badly affected by dust, so it is wise to remove those items, too, or, at the very least, cover them.

- **Establish at the outset the standards of working practice you expect.** Assign a secure place where tools and materials can be stored overnight. Make it clear that you would like the site left in a reasonable degree of tidiness at the end of each working day. If your builder prefers to work to music and the blaring radio affects your concentration, say so – don't suffer in silence. If the work requires scaffolding, make sure that ladders are removed or locked at the end of the day to prevent break-ins at upper windows.

- **Plan ahead.** Find out when the greatest disruption is likely to take place so you can make alternative arrangements. Many types of conversion necessitate interruptions to servicing – water, electricity or gas supply – which may be limited or more extensive in duration. You may need to move out for a while in the case of longer periods. Similarly, there is a stage in every conversion project when it is going to get worse before it gets better. Demolition, hacking off plaster, new brickwork, blockwork and concreting generate stupendous amounts of dust, dirt and debris. Tell yourself your home won't look like a bombsite for ever.

- **Familiarize yourself with the likely sequence of work** (see pages 38–9), even if you are not taking on a coordinator's role.

- **Be on hand to inspect the work at an agreed time of the day.** This is when you can discuss progress, identify any possible problems or make decisions if there are options. The rest of the time, keep out of the way. Clients who hover anxiously, asking questions and making less than helpful suggestions are unnecessarily distracting.

- **Resist the temptation to change your mind and up the specification at every turn.** There is no better way of finding yourself seriously out of pocket and running over schedule.

- **Be prepared for the unexpected.** Most construction jobs are likely throw up at least one surprise. Keep a level head, think laterally and be grateful for your contingency allowance.

- **Be tolerant.** It's not your builder's fault if the weather takes a serious turn for the worse or if a supplier goes out of business.

- **If all else fails and you find yourself in a dispute with your builder (or architect, subcontractor or supplier), don't fly off the handle.** Take the time to establish the facts, put your complaints in writing and arrange a meeting to talk it through. If you still can't come to an agreement, it's time to consult your solicitor or to fire your builder.

- **Spot the warning signs and take action sooner rather than later.** Evidence of bad workmanship, long periods of inactivity (especially if accompanied by a succession of implausible excuses) and other signs of incompetence indicate that you may have been unlucky in your choice. Waiting to see if things improve is not the answer.

SAFETY FIRST

It is your builder's responsibility to maintain a safe and tidy site, but you should also be aware of the potential hazards, particularly if there are young children or pets in the household.

- **Keep children well away from the action.** Do not allow them to play with tools, climb ladders or investigate any of the other potentially fascinating grown-up 'toys' lying around. When the serious construction is under way, it may be advisable to arrange for the children to stay away from home for a while. Restrict pets to closed areas where they cannot get hurt or wander off, or board them out.

- **All toxic chemicals – including paints, varnishes, seals and the like – should be kept under lock and key when not in use.**

- **Always use circuit breakers with electrical equipment.**

- **When splashed on the skin, concrete, mortar and cement dust can cause serious burns if not washed off immediately.**

- **Keep a basic first-aid kit to hand to deal with any minor injuries that may occur.**

Groundwork Employing others

Building sites may look haphazard at times, but there is a clear order in which things should be done. The art of running a project successfully lies in making sure that everything dovetails neatly – so the bathroom fixtures have been delivered by the time the plumber comes to fit them, to use a simple example. On any but the most basic projects, people will come and go, with subcontractors such as plumbers and electricians carrying out preliminary work at the 'first fix' stage, then returning at 'second fix' to complete the job once other aspects have progressed. Depending on the nature of the scheme, there may also be official inspection points when the work has to be passed and signed off by a building inspector.

If you are going to be overseeing the work yourself, rather than employing an architect or main contractor to do it for you, you need to be fully informed about what should happen when, so you can keep everything on track and ticking over smoothly. Projects suffer delay for many reasons – bad weather can bring work on foundations to a temporary halt, for example – but a project manager's role is to prevent avoidable delay as far as possible, which means thinking ahead and planning rigorously. If the electrician you booked to lay the cabling shows up on site and the trenches aren't yet dug because no one has been keeping an eye on the programme, that is avoidable delay and it will generally cost you money as well as time.

The following summary outlines the key stages in a typical building programme. Every scheme is different and you won't necessarily have to go through all these stages, particularly if works are restricted to internal areas. The stages that normally have to be passed by a building inspector are indicated.

Legalities and permissions
Depending on the nature of the scheme, you may need to obtain necessary permissions before work can begin. The major hurdle is planning permission (see Legalities and permissions, pages 41–3, to find out which type of conversions require it). If the conversion involves altering services, such as laying new connections, you will also need to contact the appropriate utility before the start of your programme. Proceeding without permission, where it is required, is illegal.

Site preparation
A wide range of different activities fall under the general heading of preparation. In the case of indoor works, preparation may involve clearing furniture and anything moveable, valuable and breakable from rooms, and putting down dustsheets and other protective coverings, right through to demolishing partitions, hacking off plasterwork and removing and disposing of existing fixtures and fittings, such as sinks or bathtubs. Externally, preparation involves clearing the ground, demolishing any unwanted existing extensions or outbuildings, putting up scaffolding and removing roof coverings.

Exterior groundworks INSPECTION STAGE
New ground-level extensions require foundations, which first means digging trenches for footings and service connections. Once the foundations have been laid, they will need to be passed by a building inspector before they are covered up. Basement conversions also require extensive groundworks and excavation.

Damp-proof course INSPECTION STAGE
After the foundations are built up to ground level, the damp-proof course is laid.

Drains and services INSPECTION STAGE
Pipework is laid for new drains; connections are made to external services, such as electricity, gas and telephone; and channels are installed for underfloor heating. Trenches cannot be covered up until drains have been tested and inspected.

Ground-floor structure INSPECTION STAGE
In most ground-level extensions, the floor structure is composed of a concrete slab. Like other external works, this stage is vulnerable to bad weather, particularly as concrete needs time to cure or harden.

Above-ground structure
This is when the walls begin to go up. Depending on the type of design, the structure may be brickwork, blockwork, steel-frame or timber-frame. Once it is complete, the roof can be covered and the extension will be less vulnerable to bad weather. In some loft conversions the roof structure may need to be strengthened and dormers constructed. Where there are new external openings or openings in load-bearing internal walls, a structural member such as beam or RSJ (rolled-steel joist) will be installed.

First fix
Subcontractors, such as carpenters, electricians and plumbers, come in to carry out a range of preliminary works, such as installing doors and window frames, glazing windows and doors, making internal partitions, laying floor joists, constructing staircases, routing wiring and internal pipework, plastering and installing boilers.

Second fix
Subcontractors return – in many cases working around each other – to install bathroom and kitchen fittings, radiators, switches, power points and lights. Second-fix carpentry includes the fitting of internal woodwork, doors, fitted storage, and kitchen and bathroom units.

Decoration
The final hands-on stage of the proceedings sees the installation of final finishes and decoration, including tilework, painting, papering and, lastly, flooring.

Completion INSPECTION STAGE
Once the works are completed, the building inspector will visit to make a final inspection. If you have hired an architect to provide a full service, he or she will inspect the job, noting any defects. The final contract sum will be due to the contractor once all the defects have been put right and approved ('snagging').

Legalities and permissions

Building work is subject to a wide range of legislation, and for very good reasons. Some types of conversion require planning permission before you can proceed at all. These tend to be alterations that could have a significant impact on the immediate environment – the appearance of the street frontage, for instance, or the spatial quality of neighbouring properties. Many other projects, especially those that require major changes to servicing, such as making new connections, or those that entail structural alteration, will need to be approved, often in stages, by a local building inspector to ensure that the work conforms to agreed standards.

Whatever you may think of individual planning decisions, the process is designed to protect the character of local communities, to retain employment opportunities where jobs are in short supply and generally to take the broad picture into account. In short, it is for everyone's long-term benefit. Building regulations are concerned with health and safety, insulation standards, structural integrity, fire protection and a host of other issues that could affect you and your immediate neighbours on a very direct basis.

Planning guidelines and laws governing construction vary from area to area and are also subject to change. Environmental considerations, for example, have led to an increase in standards required for insulation, which will affect any new extensions whether the existing house meets such criteria or not. Similarly, the latest energy regulations stipulate that a minimum of one in four light fittings (or luminaires) in extensions or converted areas should be energy-efficient. In planning, certain guidelines tend to apply across the board, while other factors – for example, the balance of residential to commercial property across the borough – are more locally determined.

A great deal of planning legislation is concerned with the impact that any changes you are proposing will have on surrounding properties and the immediate neighbourhood, particularly with respect to the appearance of street frontages.

PLANNING PERMISSION

If you employ an architect, he or she will be able to design a scheme so that it is more likely to win approval than not, and to argue its merits if it does meet with resistance. If you don't employ an architect, it is up to you to contact your local planning office, find out what is permitted and adjust your plans accordingly. As is the case with other types of legislation, ignorance is no excuse. Every year, knowingly or not, people carry out works to their home without gaining the necessary approvals. They may imagine that their conversion will somehow slip by unnoticed, or they may simply be unprepared to wait for permission and assume that they can get around to the necessary bureaucracy later. Don't be tempted by this route. If you proceed with a conversion without gaining approval, it is well within the local authority's rights to insist that the work is reversed at your own expense, particularly if it infringes guidelines or neighbours have reasonable grounds for complaint.

It is best to start the planning process by visiting your local planning department and having an informal chat with the officer who deals with your area. He or she should be able to advise you broadly on what is acceptable and what is likely to meet with objections, and may even be able to give you some advice about the type of materials that are preferred as well as general issues with respect to style. Some local authorities, it must be said, adopt a fairly conservative approach and are keen that any new developments should blend in with the surrounding area as much as possible. This is often the case in small towns with a historic character or in rural communities, but it can also be true in large cities, particularly if you live in a conservation area. Many striking contemporary conversions do get built, however, and if your taste tends in that direction, you may be fortunate enough to find a planning officer who welcomes such an approach. Whichever is the case, factor the recommendations you are given into your proposals – a small degree of compromise over window sizing or external cladding can go a long way towards smoothing the path to approval.

At the same time, you should let your neighbours know what you are planning to do. Of course, you don't have to have a full-scale consultation if you are putting in a new kitchen or moving a few internal walls around – though they may appreciate forewarning about an increase in noise and mess during the construction period. But if your conversion does require planning consent, try to keep your neighbours informed about your proposals from the outset. There is a good reason for this. The planning process allows a period of time for objections to be made, and the less your neighbours know about your plans, the more likely they are to worry that they will be adversely affected, even if that will not be the case. Getting on the right side of your neighbours is also a good idea if your conversion entails building onto a party wall or within a certain minimum distance from the boundary, which will require a party-wall award. In this context, it is worth bearing in mind that while there is no 'right to a view', there is a right to light. If your scheme will lower the levels of natural light in an adjacent property to a significant extent, it will almost certainly be refused.

The reason for preparing the ground so thoroughly is to avoid too much delay. If you have consulted with the planning officers and reassured your neighbours, your scheme should not get stuck in the system for too long. If you haven't thought things through properly or taken recommendations on board, you are more likely to be facing a protracted period of redesign and resubmission, which can extend into months and months. Even with the best will in the world, though, planners are not noted for speed and in some areas the backlog of submissions means that your scheme may take a good while to come up for consideration.

The following types of home conversion require planning permission:

- **Any alteration that involves changing the shape of your roof.**

- **An attic conversion that involves adding a dormer to the front or side of your home.** Dormers at the rear, provided they are within a certain size, do not require permission.

- **Dividing your home in such a way as to provide two separate residences, each with street access.**

- **Building onto party walls shared with neighbours or within a certain specified distance from property boundaries.**

- **Alterations to listed buildings or buildings situated in conservation areas**, particularly if these entail changes to elevations.

- **Adding an extra storey at the top of your home or on top of an existing extension.**

- **Extending your home at ground level in such a way that it increases the volume (cubic capacity) of your home by more than 10 per cent**. Also, extending beyond a specified distance or above a specified height.

- **Any conversion that involves change of use**, either from industrial and commercial to residential, or the other way round.

BUILDING REGULATIONS

If planning guidelines are often concerned with the broad picture, building regulations or 'code' get down to the nitty-gritty. The minutiae of such legislation can sometimes be a source of frustration, especially if they have an impact on style and choice of construction materials, but it is important to remember that these standards have been framed to ensure your safety and the structural integrity of your home – in other words, they represent 'best practice' as it is currently understood. If your conversion requires building regulations approval and it is not granted, even for a minor infringement, strictly speaking the works are not legal. This may not affect you directly, but when you come to sell your home it could deter a potential buyer. It may also invalidate any future insurance claim.

Like planning laws, building codes vary from area to area. In Britain legislation governs structural matters, such as foundation design and construction, along with drainage, insulation, ventilation, means of escape, fire protection and damp-proofing. A building inspector will need to view your initial plans and may indicate at this stage whether changes are required. Subsequently, the works will be inspected as they progress. Approval is granted after all the inspections have been passed.

Where building regulations can lag behind trends in design or construction is in the general area of eco-friendly building. If you are determined to use materials such as straw bale or adobe in the construction of an extension, or wish to install an environmentally friendly type of insulation, you may have a struggle on your hands to convince the powers that be that such materials will provide the necessary degree of structural integrity or fire resistance. Pioneers in eco design have often had to challenge local codes before they could put their principles into practice. In Britain, for example, timber-frame structures faced a great deal of opposition for many years, but are now considered much more favourably.

Whether or not you require planning permission for your conversion, if the work involves structural alterations, it will need to be approved by a building inspector.

Strict controls govern the design of staircases. Fire protection, detailing such as handrails and angle of pitch are some of the issues addressed by building regulations.

Other points to consider include:

- **All staircases must have handrails.** This is a particular bone of contention with many contemporary interior designers who prefer a more minimal approach to detailing.

- **If the works require new drains, these must be tested and inspected before they are covered up.** If you overlook this inspection stage, the building inspector is within his or her rights to insist that the freshly laid concrete is dug up.

- **New soil stacks must be extended a given distance above windows.**

- **Fire regulations can affect the design of staircases.** In houses over three storeys high, stairs must be 'protected', or separated from the spaces they connect. This is a particular consideration for attic conversions.

- **All 'habitable' rooms must have a window.** Kitchens and bathrooms do not count as 'habitable' rooms and can be internal, but they must be ventilated with mechanical extract.

The pace of life is rapidly accelerating and today we demand that our homes serve very different functions from just a few decades ago. The type of technological changes that have brought us wireless connections and networked computing are part of the equation. So, too, are shifts in lifestyle that have seen homes become, on the one hand, places of retreat where we can recharge our batteries and enjoy our leisure time; and on the other, with the continued trend for working at home, places of business. Flexible, multipurpose space that can be readily adapted to suit different needs is increasingly what's required.

2 New for old

Spatial planning

Many of our homes are arranged to conform to superannuated ideas of what domestic life should be, and are laid out as a series of separate rooms, each with its own notional use. Conversion doesn't always need to be about increasing space per se – it can also mean making available space more workable, more practical and more in tune with contemporary preferences for light and airy surroundings.

The type of conversions covered in the following pages concern alterations that improve the quality of existing space, but that does not mean structural issues do not come into it. If you plan to move walls around, improve access to outdoor areas, install new windows and make changes to servicing, you're still going to need professional help and advice.

In older properties, particularly those Victorian, Edwardian and prewar terraces that form the bulk of the housing stock in Britain, how you are supposed to use each individual room is generally clear. Bedrooms are at the top of the house, living areas are downstairs or at the front, kitchens are below or at the rear. This hierarchy of use separates the working or functional parts of the home from the areas devoted to relaxation or public display. But many of us don't live like that any more, so the first step is to decide whether the way space is allocated in your home matches your own preferences and needs.

Consider where you spend the most time. Family life increasingly revolves around the kitchen these days, so a large inclusive kitchen that also serves as an eating area, a place to do homework and an occasional home office may represent a better use of space than a large living area.

On the other hand, if you live alone and cook infrequently, you may wish to shrink your kitchen facilities down to the minimum and use the extra space for something you really need or want – a bigger bathroom, for example, or a dedicated home office.

If your home is arranged over several storeys, you might also think about turning the layout upside down. Semi-basement or lower-ground-floor areas are generally dark and poorly lit. Since bedrooms are used chiefly at night, it can make sense to reallocate space so that living areas move up a floor or two, where they will benefit from a better quality of natural light. How much natural light a room or area receives is not governed simply by the size or number of windows. Instead, it is a result of what's called the 'sky factor' or how much sky is visible. With lower-level windows the sky is likely to occupy only a very narrow margin at the top.

Basic practicality is also affected by circulation patterns, or how you move from area to area. Are routes clear and direct or

Removing partition walls that separate circulation spaces – halls, landings and stairs – from other areas in the home won't necessarily gain you much more space as such, but the effect will be more open and airy.

An overscaled minimally detailed opening offers the best of both worlds – the sense of free-flowing space balanced by a hint of separation.

Changes of level are a good way of suggesting a shift of activity in an otherwise open-plan area.

do you constantly encounter obstacles when performing routine tasks, such as taking out the rubbish or bringing in the shopping? If there is more than one doorway providing access to a room, which one do you use?

Lastly, think about spatial quality. Do you prefer an open-plan layout, where most daily activities are accommodated in a single multipurpose space? Or do you require a greater degree of separation and privacy? Open spaces are very appealing – they feel spacious, generous and hospitable. On the down side, they can be noisy and hard to heat. And where different household members are sharing the same space at the same time, but engaging in varied

activities, inevitably someone is going to suffer. Often a compromise is called for, with open areas balanced by more private retreats. Think about which activities might coexist most happily.

OPENING UP

Removing internal walls to create an open multipurpose space is a very common form of conversion. Options for change include removing walls that separate adjoining rooms or going further and taking down walls that enclose halls and stairs, so circulation space can be absorbed into the new layout. How much disruption, expense and complexity the work will entail depends entirely on whether the walls in question are structural or not.

In many homes walls are either simple partitions, which merely divide space but play no supporting role, or structural, which means they help to hold up your house. If you knock a big hole in a structural wall or take it down completely, you need to put in a compensatory element such as a steel beam or concrete lintel above the opening to take the weight the wall had been supporting. Don't be tempted to guess whether a wall is structural or not. Get advice from a professional, who will also be able to recommend the right size of beam or lintel to put in its place.

If your home is relatively featureless, the sweep of open space that results from such an alteration will look reasonably natural. If, however, you live in a period property with architectural detailing, it may be best to go for a semi-open layout that retains a hint of separation. For example, knocking through a terraced house from front to back can expose two

A contemporary update on the traditional kitchen serving hatch, this elongated opening provides a view through to the dining area while screening kitchen activity.

A well-judged internal opening in a partition wall that stops short of the ceiling allows the space to read as one, while marking a separation of activities.

chimney breasts and fireplaces lined up on the same wall. The answer here might be to opt for a large or overscaled opening, rather than remove the dividing wall altogether. You can always size such an opening to suit double doors, which would allow you to separate the spaces in future if you wanted to.

A sense of openness can also be generated without knocking down walls left, right and centre. Internal openings, such as judiciously placed doors and internal windows, can reveal new sightlines and vistas that lead the eye from place to place while retaining a degree of separation. Such changes can be particularly beneficial if you have an internal kitchen or bathroom, because they will inevitably improve the quality of natural light in such areas by borrowing it from elsewhere. New internal windows can be any shape – round portholes, horizontal or vertical strips, or squares – and can be left open or filled with clear, translucent or coloured glass. In the same way, new internal doorways can be designed to conform with existing doors or take the form of overscaled panels or sliding screens running from floor to ceiling. Translucent materials such as glass and Perspex spread available light around. As is the case with removing entire walls, removing portions of walls to create such openings may entail structural work if the wall in question is load-bearing.

DIVIDING UP

Spatial rearrangement occasionally requires the construction of new dividing walls or partitions. Unless you are moving a load-bearing wall to a new position, structural issues do not come into play.

Putting up a partition is straightforward work that simply consists of constructing a stud framework and then covering it with plasterboard.

Even quite minimal changes to the position of a partition wall can deliver big benefits. Blocking up a redundant doorway, for example, can give you more wall space to play with on both sides of the divide. In the case of kitchens and other fitted spaces, such a change can make all the difference between a practical working layout and one that falls somewhat short of basic efficiency. Bathrooms are another case in point. If your bathroom is very small, moving the wall that divides it from the hall or landing forward a short distance can vastly improve the potential layout of fixtures and fittings.

When you are dividing one large space into two – perhaps to give each child in the family their own bedroom – you need to think about the position of windows and how each space will subsequently be accessed. Ideally, the new wall should create two new areas that are roughly equivalent in size, each with a window. Organizing access can be a little more problematic and some space may need to be sacrificed from adjacent landings or halls in order to create individual doors to each new room.

New partition walls do not have to run in straight lines. Curves, especially if you are enclosing a bathroom or similar service area, can be very dynamic. A staggered partition that creates an alcove in each new room can be an effective way of providing areas for fitted storage.

Half-height or half-width partitions are also an invaluable way of underscoring a shift of activity in an open-plan area. A low counter screening a kitchen from a living area in a multipurpose layout, for example, disguises food preparation while doubling up as a breakfast bar. A half-width partition can provide just enough psychological separation to enclose a work area within a living room without blocking natural light completely or undermining the openness of the space.

ABOVE
A translucent glass panel partially obscures views of a bathroom while letting light through.

LEFT
Bi-folding floor-to-ceiling doors provide flexible spatial arrangement. Taking doorways right up to the ceiling is much neater than retaining a small margin of wall over the lintel.

Enlarging an external opening that connects to the garden or creating a new one is a good way of taking the indoors closer to the outdoors. The sense of seamless transition in this case is achieved by making sure the levels are the same on both sides of the opening, effectively annexing the terrace in fine weather.

BRINGING THE OUTSIDE IN

Improving the way interior spaces relate to the world outside can have a massive impact on spatial quality. Older properties dating back a century or so often tend to turn their backs on outdoor spaces. Access may be poor – in urban areas back gardens may have been viewed primarily as service areas rather than green retreats. Or windows may be small, which is often the case in older country cottages and houses.

The modern desire for light and airy surroundings can be difficult to satisfy without making some changes to external walls. We increasingly prefer to treat our gardens as extensions of interior spaces – outdoor living rooms, where we can take advantage of good weather to cook, relax and entertain in the open air. Aesthetics aside, ensuring a smooth, free-flowing connection from indoors to out gives you the practical means to make full use of the garden. Stepping straight from a living room or kitchen into the garden, rather than having to negotiate a flight of steps or track through a back room, immediately brings the outside closer to the interior.

At the same time, enlarging openings or adding new windows or doors improves the quality of natural light, which in turn enhances the sense of space. The better an interior is lit, the more uplifting it will

be. Large openings, such as sliding glass panels or doors, generate a great feeling of expansiveness.

In almost all cases, making changes to external walls necessitates structural work. The exception is lengthening existing windows. If you remove the portion of wall under the lower cill, perhaps to turn a window into a door, you do not have to install a compensatory element such as a beam or lintel. But if you widen a window or door – to make French doors, for example – or if you create new openings, a beam, joist or lintel will need to be installed across the top of the opening to take the weight of the structure above.

Pay particular attention to the siting and design of a new opening. Orientation affects the quality of natural light, with west- or south-facing aspects giving a warmer light, and north- and east-facing aspects a cooler one. At the same time, windows admit views as well as light, and you will gain little benefit from a new opening if it faces a neighbouring brick wall or results in an unwelcome loss of privacy. The rear of your property may offer more scope for changes to external walls than the front, particularly if you live in an area where the houses are all of a similar type or date from the same period. In some cases, changing a front elevation, by altering windows and doors or by adding new openings, may not be permitted by the local authority. This will almost certainly be the case in a conservation area. However, what would appear too radical from the street – a solid wall replaced with floor-to-ceiling sliding glass doors, for instance – would raise no eyebrows at the back and would effectively dissolve the boundary between outdoors and in.

Extending the same type of flooring material outside, or at least using flooring of a similar type and tone, will help to link indoors and out in a visual sense. Where polished wooden floorboards meet decking, or stone meets stone, the eye will be tricked into reading the space as one, even though there is a separation between the two.

Two final points to consider are the impact of larger or more numerous openings on internal temperature control and on security. Expanses of glazing can result in overheating in warm weather and plummeting temperatures in colder months. If you are considering extensive glazing, it can be well worth exploring the eco alternatives. Low-E (or low-emissivity) glass has a special coating that prevents excessive heat loss; it is more expensive, but in the long term you will save on your heating bills. Choose toughened

ABOVE
Blurring the boundaries between indoors and out provides the opportunity to design outdoor spaces that read as extensions of the house. This pathway leading from the glazed kitchen door takes the eye right through the garden.

RIGHT
A glazed wall inset with doors separates this soaring double-height space from the garden, letting daylight flood in. The framed panes of glass are as effective as but less structurally demanding than expanses of sheet glass.

OVERLEAF
Enlarging an opening to create a glazed end wall is structural work. A joist or other structural member needs to be inserted to compensate for the missing portion of load-bearing wall.

shatterproof glass that fractures into harmless pebbles for any large glazed opening to reduce the risk of accidents. There is also special glass with built-in sensors that triggers an alarm system in the case of an attempted break-in.

In spatial terms, most of us don't have a problem thinking laterally. With a little practice, it is easy enough to find your way around a floor plan and imagine different configurations of layout. Thinking vertically – in terms of section – is a different matter. It is in this department that architects and spatial designers truly excel. Changes to the 'volume' of your home can be the most dramatic of all and can completely transform your experience of a space.

Volume, or the three-dimensional aspect of a given area, takes into account height as well as length and breadth. In many houses all rooms have more or less the same ceiling height and the staircase is the only place where different levels can be experienced. Varying volumes – so that small, enclosed areas give way to soaring double-height spaces – introduces a whole new dynamic.

Top lighting – that is, installing windows at a high level or in the roof – literally lifts off the lid. In terms of volume, the sky's the limit. Glazed roofs, skylights, rooflights and high-level windows have the ultimate 'sky factor', bathing an interior in a flood of light and exposing it to all the subtle and evocative variations in light levels throughout the day. Think carefully about where you site the opening to gain maximum impact from the change.

You will need to consult an engineer or surveyor to determine whether any structural work is necessary. Inserting

Dividing up space vertically provides the opportunity for dynamic internal views and the option for bringing light down from roof glazing into the lower levels.

a window into the roof increases the load on the roof structure and in most cases surrounding rafters will need to be doubled up to take the additional load. Fully glazed roofs need careful specification and detailing to make sure that they are both properly supported and fully waterproof.

There is also maintenance to consider. Gazing up at the sky through a puddle of dirty water does not brighten anyone's day. Many commercially available roof windows pivot for easy cleaning. Self-cleaning glass that encourages water run-off is also available; alternatively, glazed roofs can be canted at a slight angle so that rainwater does not collect on top.

You will also need to consult your local planning department to see whether there are any restrictions that govern this type of change. In some areas rooflights and other types of top glazing do not require permission if they are installed at the rear or side of the building. Where top lighting would affect the appearance of the front elevation, however, it may be more strictly controlled.

The impact of top lighting can be further exploited by changes to internal levels that open up your home vertically. Sacrificing a portion of floor so that light spills down through two or more levels is one way of doing it. Another, which is becoming increasingly popular, is to replace a section of solid floor with floor-level glazing. Various types of glass are suitable for this use, including a new variety that incorporates a fine metal mesh. Again, detailing and specification is critical and you will need specialist advice from the supplier or a design professional.

New for old   Spatial planning

Our homes must fulfil many different functions today. At the same time, pressure on space is increasing. The result is that many of us live in homes that are a little bit smaller than we would like. One solution is to enlarge the size of your home by extending it in some way or converting a redundant area. But if your budget won't stretch that far or if other practical limitations rule out those options, building in a degree of flexibility can help to ease the pressure on space.

When your home is a tight squeeze, some areas are going to have to serve multiple functions to ease the pressure. Workable combinations include related activities – cooking and eating, for example. Similarly, bathing and sleeping share a basic requirement for privacy. Fully open-plan layouts accommodate everything from watching television to entertaining friends to lunch within the same space. Building in as much as possible behind the scenes not only makes such multipurpose areas work better, it also makes them visually more comfortable.

One important function that our homes must fulfil is to serve as a repository for our belongings and the accoutrements of everyday life – pots and pans, media equipment, gardening tools, records and documents. Neatly designed working walls of fitted storage are much less visually intrusive and can house vast amounts of clutter. At the same time, such an arrangement can enable you to slot in fold-down or pull-out tables and beds, freeing up floor space. Panels or screens that pull out can subdivide space for additional privacy or demarcate a working area within a general living space. Very ingenious fitted solutions allow for many different functional permutations – the ultimate in transformable living.

These types of changes cannot be approached piecemeal. You will need the advice of an architect or interior designer who specializes in this type of work. Standards of construction must also be high – fitted areas need to work seamlessly or they will be a constant source of frustration.

Building in flexibility makes the fullest use of available space. Some neat solutions for mopping up clutter include: fitting drawers into stair treads; converting an understairs space into an additional seating area; installing a workstation into an alcove; and making use of undereaves space for fitted drawers.

Changes to servicing

The basic infrastructure of your home comprises various lines of supply: electricity, gas, water and drainage, as well as lines of communication. Changing services is disruptive and tends to involve the kind of work that means floors and floor coverings need to be taken up and channels dug in plasterwork, so unless there is an emergency, or the current infrastructure cannot meet present needs or is positively unsafe, most people are content to leave well enough alone.

If, however, you are already embarking on a medium- to large-scale conversion project, it makes good sense to take the opportunity to review the infrastructure of your home at the same time and possibly upgrade it. Flexible living is best supported by an increased number of power points, so that electrical equipment can be used in any part of the space. You may also wish to consider incorporating concealed lighting or underfloor heating on the grounds of saving space or to provide a neat, less intrusive look. Other types of conversion may necessitate changes to servicing to improve a kitchen or bathroom layout, for example, or to extend services to a new area.

Planning changes to servicing and carrying out the work are both strictly jobs for the professionals. You may also require the approval of the relevant utility and/or your local building inspector. For obvious reasons, very strict regulations govern nearly every aspect related to basic domestic service provision, from the permitted height of power points above the floor, to the ventilation of boilers and the siting of soil stacks. Failing to meet these regulations may compromise your health and the safety of your property –

it may even be lethal. Connecting to a mains supply – whether it is gas, water or electricity – is always the job of the utility or relevant board.

As eco awareness climbs higher up the agenda, changing services can enable you to do your bit for the environment while saving money on maintenance costs. Upgrading to an energy-efficient boiler, for example, can cut fuel bills dramatically. Investing in a solar-energy system or a wind turbine can deliver significant environmental benefits over the long term. Check with your planning department first: permission will generally be required if you intend to site solar panels or wind turbines on your roof.

It is cheaper and less disruptive if you can work with existing servicing runs rather than reroute them around your home. Changes to services require official approval and possibly the input of the relevant utility or board.

ELECTRICITY

In Britain power is generally routed around the home in a number of circuits, each of which is fused. In any given area power points will be on one circuit, lighting on another and there will also be single circuits for appliances such as cookers.

Points to consider:
- Any change to your electrical arrangements, even the most basic, should be carried out by a qualified electrician who has professional accreditations.
- If your wiring is more than 15 years old, it probably needs to be replaced. If possible, schedule the upgrade at a time when you are planning other major works.
- Fuses that blow repeatedly often indicate that there is a fault in a particular circuit.
- Many homes, especially those that date back to Victorian or Edwardian times, have far too few power points. This not only limits room arrangement unnecessarily, it can also be dangerous. Overloaded sockets and trailing cables are potential hazards.
- Power points don't have to be fitted to walls. You can have sockets installed in the floor, too, which adds to the flexibility of spatial use.
- If you are replacing lighting wiring or putting a lighting circuit into an extension or converted space, new regulations stipulate that a minimum of one in four fittings must be energy-efficient, which in practice tends to mean those fittings that take fluorescent lamps.

HEATING

Whether your heating is powered by gas, electricity, oil or some other fuel, by far the most common arrangement in Britain is the wet system, where water is heated by a boiler and fed to radiators around the home. Generally, water is fed from a cold-water cistern to a hot-water cylinder via the boiler where it is heated, though combination boilers heat water directly from the mains supply. A more expensive heating system, though increasingly common, is underfloor heating, where the heating elements are located underneath the floor.

Points to consider:
- Increasing the volume of your home by converting an attic or basement, or by adding an extension will put extra demands on your boiler. Consult a heating engineer to see if you need to upgrade. You may also need advice on the optimum siting of radiators.
- Condensing boilers, which reclaim heat from exhaust gases, are the most energy-efficient.
- Underfloor heating can be used in combination with many flooring materials, including wood, but it is most efficient with thermally massive materials such as concrete and stone, which absorb and release heat slowly.
- The latest thermostatic controls or boiler managers 'learn' your patterns of use, so heating comes on only when you need it. Individual controls let you set radiators at different levels of heat in different areas.
- Regulations govern the position of meters, boilers, flues and exhaust vents, and boiler ventilation, as well as the type of pipes and wiring and their routing.

Alterations to drainage are potentially the most disruptive of all, which is an important factor to bear in mind when you are planning changes to kitchens and bathrooms. For example, it is much easier to create a new bathroom on a level either directly above or directly below an existing one, rather than on the opposite side of the house.

In Britain clean drinking water generally enters the home from the water main in the street via a rising main that routes water both to a cold-water cistern (often located in the attic) and to the cold kitchen tap. This supply is controlled both by a stopcock inside the house and by a water board stopcock outside, between the water main and rising main. All the other cold taps are fed by pipes from the cistern and for this reason the water is not, strictly speaking, drinkable. Lavatories and the hot-water cylinder are also fed from the cold-water cistern.

Waste water and sewage from lavatories drains either to the main sewer via ground-level drains or to a septic tank underground (an arrangement more common in rural areas). Sewage from lavatories above ground level enters a ventilated soil stack that feeds into the main drains. Water-sealed trapped gullies feed into the drains to prevent smells.

Points to consider:
- Pipework that routes waste water to the drains must be laid to a fall, in order to prevent blockages. Where there is insufficient fall, pipes are more likely to silt up.
- Simple plumbing layouts are less likely to cause trouble than pipework that is overly complicated, with many branched connections and changes of direction.
- Make sure that you know where the stopcock is, so you can turn off the mains supply in the case of an emergency.
- Major alterations to drainage, as well as new drains, need to be approved by the local building inspector.

Generous bathrooms allow for more dynamic spatial arrangements. Here pipework is built in behind panelling, with the bath treated almost as a piece of furniture rather than a fixture.

New kitchens and bathrooms

Kitchens and bathrooms are the two areas in the home most likely to see radical makeovers – improvements that go beyond the simply cosmetic, involving changes to layout and perhaps to servicing as well. In both cases, fitted or semi-fitted solutions are often preferred, while there will undoubtedly be some fixed points in the layout to take into account. For all these reasons – not to mention the fact that both kitchens and bathrooms tend to be in daily use – these types of conversion projects can be very demanding.

There are many specialist outlets that can help you to design, plan and carry out a kitchen or bathroom conversion. These range from mass-market retailers or special design and fitting services within superstores to high-end bespoke designers and suppliers. For an individual look, you could also seek the advice of an architect or interior designer who is prepared to tackle a relatively small project.

Points to consider:
- Whichever route you choose, it's important to get it all down on paper first. Scale plans are invaluable, as a way of both assessing what you've got and of determining where change is required (see page 23).
- Work with existing servicing arrangements as far as possible to minimize disruption and expense. If you need to move servicing around to improve the workability of the layout, always seek professional advice to see if what you are planning is legal and feasible.

- Focus on basic practicality before you go on to choose individual fittings, cabinetry or finishes. In practice, this means spending time working out the optimal layout. Both kitchens and bathrooms must function effectively to be any use at all – style is an irrelevance if you are constantly frustrated when carrying out everyday routines.
- Think about incorporating concealed fixed lighting or underfloor heating if you are having a major overhaul.
- Choose materials and finishes that can withstand wear and tear, that are waterproof, slip-proof and easy to clean.
- Schedule the work for periods when you can better stand the inevitable disruption and make alternative arrangements while the area in question is out of commission.

Kitchen conversions can be very challenging because the space is so hardworking and there are so many diverse factors to juggle – heat and water supply, optimum layout of appliances and preparation zones, and so on.

Kitchens are hardworking areas with many potential hazards. Working with sharp utensils, dealing with heavy pans of boiling water and cooking over open flames demand conditions that are as efficient, practical and safe as possible. Layout is key. Most kitchen appliances and fitted units come in standard modules (600mm/24in wide), which makes it easy to achieve a seamless effect.

The time-honoured notion of the 'working triangle' lies at the heart of most successful kitchen planning. Based on ergonomic studies of kitchen work, this rule of thumb stipulates desirable distances between the three main centres of kitchen activity – the wet area or sink, the hot area or hob and oven, and the cold area or fridge. If these three centres are too distant from one another, you will waste too much time and energy moving between them; if they are too close, working conditions will be overly cramped. In either case, risks multiply.

The U-shaped kitchen layout is one of the most flexible and practical, giving plenty of room to manoeuvre. It does not require a vast amount of space, but is not feasible in very tight kitchens.

The working triangle can be applied to a number of common kitchen layouts, depending on how big and what shape your kitchen is. These include:

The in-line layout

Kitchens can be arranged so that all the working areas are aligned along one wall. This is a practical layout if the kitchen occupies part of a multipurpose space and you wish to screen it from view part of the time with folding doors or sliding screens, though some people find it tiring to work in.

The U-shaped layout

One of the most versatile and functional of all kitchen layouts, this arrangement is suitable for all but the smallest of kitchens. The open end of the U can be used to site a dining area.

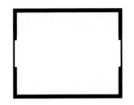

The galley layout

This is a good solution for a restricted space. Preparation and working areas occupy two facing walls with a narrow gangway between them.

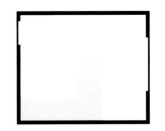

The L-shaped layout

Another good solution for a kitchen in a multipurpose space; the shorter arm of the L can serve as a room divider or breakfast bar.

The island kitchen

Some of the main kitchen functions are accommodated in an island in the centre of the layout. This type of arrangement generally requires plenty of space.

BATHROOM LAYOUTS

There is no equivalent to the working triangle when it comes to bathroom layouts, but an overriding consideration is to provide some physical and psychological separation between the lavatory and the bath/shower and basin. This can be achieved by siting the lavatory on the wall opposite the bath/shower and by making sure that the head of the bath is not aligned with the lavatory. Half-height or half-width partitions can also be used to screen the two fixtures from one another.

The size, shape and style of bathroom fixtures vary widely. For most people, size will be an important factor, particularly if their bathroom is tight. Awkward room shapes can also be accommodated with corner fittings or curved ones.

Treating the bathroom as a fully fitted space is a good way of resolving the inherent differences of scale and contour between bath, basin and lavatory. With wall-hung or built-in fixtures and the spaces between filled with concealed fitted storage, the room reads better as a whole. Really generous bathrooms, on the other hand, can serve almost as living areas, with a tub placed in the centre of the space or projected at right angles from the wall. A third option is the wet room, where a shower drains directly to an outlet sunk in the floor and there is no separate shower tray. These must be carefully constructed and specified so they are fully waterproof.

LEFT

A beautifully detailed bathroom makes the most of limited space, with its walk-in shower minimally screened by glazing and bath inset into a fitted unit with sinks at either end.

BELOW

On a more generous scale, this bathroom features a tub raised on blocks, with free access at either end.

Converting period properties

In Britain, where a substantial proportion of the housing stock is more than a century old, and some of it is much older than that, many of us live in homes with a layout, detailing and decoration that would have been familiar to our grandparents, great-grandparents and even great-great-grandparents. While not everyone wants to step back into the Victorian era every time they open their front door, obliterating the past and replacing it with cutting-edge modernity is not necessarily the way to go. Somewhere between the two extremes is an approach that preserves the character of our architectural heritage without creating a time warp that is out of step with modern lifestyles.

The term 'period property' covers a multitude of sins, as anyone acquainted with estate agents' euphemisms could tell you – anything from a humble Victorian or Edwardian terrace, of the kind that makes up a large percentage of the suburban development of many towns and cities, to exquisite Georgian rectories, half-timbered Tudor cottages and other rare survivors from the more distant past. Houses of a more recent period might also fit into this category, such as prewar semis that display flamboyant Art Deco detailing or early modernist influences.

If your home is neither listed nor in a designated conservation area, you will be permitted to do pretty much what you like to its interior – subject, of course, to the usual planning and building controls. If you want to carve out a contemporary open-plan space inside your Edwardian end-of-terrace, that is up to you. Externally, however, planners tend to be more conservative in what they permit and you may have to restrict changes, to the front elevation in particular, to those that blend in with neighbouring properties.

Listed buildings and those in conservation areas are subject to much more stringent control. The policy of 'listing' buildings to safeguard our architectural heritage began during the Second World War, when the impact of aerial bombardment focused minds on how to protect whatever would survive the Blitz. It was also a time when many of the great country houses were entering a period of decline, as upkeep became too expensive and death duties began to bite. More recently, listing has extended to other categories of building – pubs, old factories and warehouses, as well as good or early examples of particular technological developments, such as concrete construction. Buildings can either be 'spot' listed as individual examples worth preserving or may form part of a conservation area, where the intention is to maintain both architectural character and existing street patterns.

Period properties require sensitive handling. Here existing architectural detail has been painted white to match the décor.

Period properties are highly adaptable, arguably more so than homes of more recent construction. Provided your home is not listed or in a conservation area, you can extend and alter it as you please (with the usual planning and building-control provisos). Many houses built a century or more ago are more generous in scale and proportion than modern houses and apartments, for the simple reason that land was less expensive then in comparative terms. As a result of this, behind quite a number of historical façades are stunning contemporary interiors, with sweeping open-plan layouts that take full advantage of the additional volume.

Some people who live in a period home find themselves increasingly intrigued by the details and decorative styles favoured in the past. For them, 'conversion' might take the form of a loving and painstaking restoration, down to the last bell-pull and dado rail.

Historic or period character is expressed in various ways, including the style of construction, internal layout and designated room use, the use of materials, architectural detailing and, more superficially, decoration and furnishing.

If you are interested in full or partial restoration, here are some points for you to consider:

- Do your research. Costume dramas are not infallible guides to period décor, however much went into the budget. There are many specialist historical societies that can advise on typical features and plenty of books on the subject.
- Visit houses of a similar type and age. Historically, architectural detailing has been particularly vulnerable to vandalism, theft, general decay and modernization. If your house is missing its original Victorian fireplace, for example, this does not mean all the fireplaces in your street have suffered the same fate and you may be able to get an idea of what it might have looked like by visiting your neighbours.
- The more 'authentic' you wish to be, the less you can do to alter basic layout and proportion. Architectural detail is specific to the context of the interior. Knocking two rooms into one and preserving the dado rail produces an architectural mishmash.
- Good sources for period features include auctions, salvage yards and other second-hand outlets. Some suppliers do produce original detailing, such as plasterwork mouldings, in appropriate materials; others reproduce the style in lightweight plastic or polystyrene, which is generally less convincing.
- Be prepared to conceal modern amenities, such as radiators, media equipment and kitchen appliances.

Old flooring and exposed beams lend character to a bathroom fitted out with contemporary fixtures. Confident contrasts of style can be very effective when you are converting a property that has a long history.

It is probably fair to say that most people who live in period properties endeavour to meet their homes halfway, introducing the new alongside the old. This strategy is often as much about practicality as it is about taste. After all, a home does not have to be either historically accurate for its period or bang up to date – most houses have seen change over time and represent something of a compromise.

Points to consider:
- Focus on the main architectural elements rather than the more superfluous ones. The functions of details such as dado rails and picture rails are largely irrelevant these days. Keeping a decorative ceiling rose (particularly one that is damaged or in poor condition) can also create a visual anomaly if you don't intend to have a central light. Original windows and doors, on the other hand, root a building in its period and should be preserved, restored or replaced as far as possible.
- Strong contemporary surfaces and finishes can make an effective contrast to a period interior. Choice of flooring, for example, can introduce a note of modernity without taking away from the basic character of a room.
- If you are making changes to layout, such as knocking two rooms into one, either remove any details that suggest the area was once two separate spaces or retain a hint of separation.

A dramatic glazed wall adds a contemporary touch to an older terraced house. Such changes are rarely contentious in planning terms if they are made to the rear of the property. Options are much more limited at the front.

Changes to listed buildings

Listed buildings fall into three categories: Grade I, Grade II* and Grade II, with Grade I being the highest and rarest grade; 90 per cent of listed buildings are Grade II. Most listed buildings were constructed before 1840 and nearly every substantially intact building constructed before 1700 is listed. However, a house does not need to be listed to fall within additional planning control. Homes in conservation areas, defined as areas of special architectural or historic interest, are also subject to specific legislation.

Alterations that may need listed-building consent include:

- Changing windows or doors.
- Painting over brickwork or removing external finishes, such as rendering.
- Putting in dormer windows or rooflights.
- Putting up aerials, satellite dishes and burglar alarms.
- Changing roofing materials.
- Moving or removing internal walls.
- Making new doorways.
- Removing or altering fireplaces, panelling or staircases.
- Certain kinds of repair, such as repointing brickwork.

Alterations to homes in conservation areas that may require consent include:

- Changing external cladding.
- Putting in dormer windows.
- Putting up satellite dishes that are visible from the street.
- Putting up porches.
- Painting a house a different colour.
- Changing doors, windows or architectural details.
- Cutting down or lopping trees.

Ignorance of the law is no excuse and penalties can be severe if you proceed without permission – it's a criminal offence. If you want to change your home and it is listed, you should visit your local council first and speak to a conservation officer to find out whether your proposals are likely to be acceptable. Always engage a builder and/or architect who has experience of working on listed buildings and knows the type of issues that are likely to arise.

Second skins

Houses that are of a more recent date can also be given a fresh face. Many homes built in the 1950s, 1960s and 1970s are relatively unprepossessing in appearance and some are downright dull. Whatever internal works or additions you plan to bring the interior up to date, you can also upgrade the exterior and introduce a sense of quality and a contemporary edge.

In some cases, people have opted to wrap their otherwise featureless suburban boxes in wood cladding, such as larch, cedarwood or other woods that mellow with time and exposure and need little or no subsequent maintenance. The sleek, modernist results are a far cry from meretricious stone cladding or pebbledash rendering that blight many terraced streets. Improving window frames and tidying away the clutter of porches can also help to put a fresh face on things.

Changes to street elevations normally require planning permission, but if your home is not in a conservation area and is of a relatively recent date, you are unlikely to meet with many objections.

Natural timber weatherboarding and new windows add a touch of class to an otherwise unremarkable suburban house.

Case study 1

Reconstructed and replanned terraced house

Victorian terraced houses tend to be laid out in a similar way, with a number of small rooms on each level and those at the front cut off from the garden. After looking at a number of houses, the clients decided it would be more cost-effective to buy a property in need of renovation and set their budget as the likely value of the refurbished house.

In order to come up with the light-filled spacious home that the clients wanted, the architect's solution was to turn the layout upside down, and open up the whole first floor as a free-flowing space serving as kitchen, dining area and living room, connected to the back garden by a new second staircase. This left the ground floor for bedrooms and bathrooms, conceived as 'transformable space' so that different configurations are possible, depending on which doors are open or closed. The entire end wall of the house is glazed, drenching the interior with natural light.

The view of the rear wall with its expanse of glazing. A new second staircase connects the replanned first floor to the garden. Changes to first-floor structures are easier and cheaper than changes to ground floors, which helped to keep the project within budget. A clear glass balustrade separating the breakfast area at the end of the kitchen from the staircase allows views down to the deck below.

The conversion delivered the light-filled, open-plan space the clients wanted. Detailing is simple – white walls and wood floors. Victorian windows are disguised by floor-to-ceiling Venetian blinds that diffuse the light. With the addition of the second staircase, it is possible to vary routes through the house or simply move about from space to space in a continuous circuit.

In Victorian terraced houses there is a change of level between the front rooms and the rooms in the rear return. Taking advantage of this is a 7m- (23ft-) long stainless-steel kitchen counter, which forms a low coffee table in the living room and a breakfast area at the other end overlooking the garden. Kitchen appliances and equipment are concealed in fitted wall cupboards.

Case study 2

Replanned and renovated basement flat

Like many basement flats, this one was dark and poky, and arranged so there was only limited access to the garden, one of its best features. The potential for conversion was greatly increased, however, by the fact that there were few structural walls and entry was directly from the street. This meant that the spaces could be opened up without too much difficulty or expense.

The principal strategy was to flip the layout. Originally, the garden could be accessed only through one of the two bedrooms at the rear. In the new layout the living area leads directly to the garden and the main bedroom is at the front. The new spaces are oriented on a 'spine' that follows the line of the island unit and oak-veneered cupboards and extends out into the garden in the form of a decked pathway. The materials and layout of the garden design harmonize with the interior so that the distinction between the two areas is blurred.

Careful attention to detail and a high standard of finish create a clean-lined contemporary interior. The flooring throughout most of the flat is polished concrete. Beyond the dining area, panels of weathered waxed steel are wrapped around the bathroom. Oak-veneered cupboards provide storage, conceal the boiler and are fitted with bookshelves.

RIGHT
Looking through the interior towards the garden. Folding and sliding doors connect indoors and out and allow natural light to penetrate deep within the interior. The dining area is located where the bathroom used to be. A low plinth topped with limestone serves as seating; underneath are oak-veneered cupboards for electronic media and other storage.

LEFT
The open-plan kitchen features an island unit topped with stone that houses the sink, drawers and dishwasher. The other appliances are concealed behind lacquered panels on the rear wall. Beyond the light blue painted wall is a second bedroom.

Case study 3

Whole house conversion

Formerly a local authority-owned children's home, this Victorian semidetached house has been converted top to bottom to provide a bright, flexible home for an architect couple and their growing family. The first task was to strip everything down to the bare shell – most of the original features had already gone. With partitions and chimney breasts removed, what was left were three huge open-plan floors.

Connecting the levels is a new open-tread staircase supported on a steel frame cast into the wall. This is expressed on the rear elevation by a long expanse of glass, created by elongating the original windows until they formed a continuous opening. The kitchen and living areas are linked on the ground floor. The main bedroom occupies the first floor, along with a home office and living room. The top floor is given over to the children and is divided by three sliding walls, so the space can either be separated into individual bedrooms or opened out as a play area.

The new staircase is visible through a strip of window, formed by elongating the existing windows. A central steel frame threaded with thick steel wires like those used for rigging acts as a banister. Together with the open treads, this allows light through into the house.

LEFT
A striking feature of the conversion is the colour scheme. Bright green flooring extends throughout the house – studded rubber in the kitchen and a specially dyed carpet elsewhere, even on the stair treads. On the first floor a sliding wall provides privacy for the main bedroom.

BELOW
The kitchen is only minimally separated from the living areas by an open-ended spine wall. Basic storage units are mirrored to help spread the light around. The dining table is made from a steel fire door.

Loft or attic conversions have long been one of the most popular ways of gaining extra room. In Britain, where terraced streets are common and housing density is high in towns and cities, many homes lack sufficient garden space to extend at ground level. However, what many properties do have, particularly older ones, is a generous attic. When homeowners feel the pinch, it is not surprising that one of the first places where they look for additional space is right under the roof.

3 Attics

The only way is up

Like many other types of home improvement, converting a loft tends to represent better value for money than moving, once you have taken stamp duty and other moving costs into consideration. That is especially true if you simply need one extra room, rather than a substantially larger home. Similarly, in the majority of cases, what you spend getting the work done will probably be more than offset by enhanced resale value. As in other conversion projects, it is worth doing some research – ask an estate agent to estimate how much a loft conversion would add to the value of your home and make sure that your budget remains comfortably within that margin to get the best value for money and to be sure of recouping those costs should you come to sell.

ABOVE
A roof extension provides an inviting eyrie at the top of the house, along with access to a roof terrace. The sloping roofline has less impact on neighbours.

RIGHT
Most lofts can be converted these days, provided there is enough head height. Sloping roof planes are part of the appeal and create cosy intimacy.

What a loft conversion will also add to your home is character. There is something particularly appealing about roof spaces. Tucked away at the top of the house, they have a cosy, intimate quality that makes them ideal as contemplative retreats. Sloping roof planes, dormer windows and skylights give such spaces a quirky charm that is often missing from more standard box-like rooms.

Because loft conversions have been a favoured option for so long, there are now many companies that specialize exclusively in this type of work. For a truly bespoke result, you may wish to consult an architect, but for a decent all-round conversion, loft conversion specialists often represent a good bet. If you are after a simple fit-out, perhaps in order to use the attic as a storage area, a good building firm should be able to tackle the work with no difficulty.

IS IT FEASIBLE?

The first question most people ask is whether it is feasible in structural terms to convert their loft or attic. Nowadays the answer is usually yes, provided there is enough head height.

A few decades ago, converting a loft in a new or newish home was generally ruled out because of structural complications. Many modern houses have preformed roof trusses, unlike older properties where the roof structure leaves clear space underneath. However, new structural-engineering techniques can now deal successfully with the conversion of many types of roof structure, including preformed roof trusses, as well as those in timber-frame buildings, and while the work may be more involved, the result is just the same.

The critical factor is sufficient head height. In some areas regulations stipulate that at least half the floor area in the converted space must have a minimum head height of at least 2.3m (7½ft). If you stand just under the roof ridge and the distance between it and the joists below is 2.3m or over, your loft is probably convertible. The only alternative, if there is insufficient head height, is to lower the floor. This is complex building work and may impinge on the quality of rooms on the level below.

LEFT

If your loft is too small for a bedroom or living area, shifting a home office up there can have an impact on how you use space elsewhere. Being out of the way, lofts provide psychological breathing space that aids concentration.

ABOVE

A converted loft makes an excellent child's bedroom. Children particularly respond to the appeal of such quirky spaces. If a loft is going to be in regular daily use, it must have a safe and secure means of access.

Assessing your needs

How you intend to use the new loft space will have a direct bearing on the complexity of the work involved and the amount of money you will need to spend on final finishes and fitting out.

Don't just assume that because you need another bedroom, the loft should be dedicated to that use. Think about your home as a whole and how rooms and functions could be juggled to provide the optimum use of space.

Options include:

- **Using the loft for storage.**
  This involves the basic strengthening of floor joists and boarding over to create a proper storage area. This is an inexpensive and straightforward option – but it can have a massive knock-on effect, improving spatial quality immeasurably elsewhere in the home. Many lofts remain empty while the rooms below are stuffed to the gills with the overspill of life. Shift clutter into a dry, well-insulated roof space and your home will immediately function better and feel more spacious.

- **Using the loft as a bedroom.**
  But whose? A converted loft can make a self-contained retreat for a master bedroom or a welcome den for a teenager. If you equip it with rudimentary washing facilities, such as a basin, it can also form a private room for a lodger or au pair.

- **Using the loft as a home office**
  Rooflights provide a good quality of bright natural light, which is ideal for concentrated work. At the same time, lofts are away from the ordinary run of the household, which provides the essential psychological separation between home life and working life.

- **Using the loft to increase the sense of volume and improve natural light in the levels below.**
  If there is not enough head height to enable you to convert your loft into a habitable room, you might consider installing a skylight or two and removing a portion of the floor to create a sense of uplift on the level below. The remainder of the floor area could serve as a mezzanine for a high-level bed with built-in storage beneath.

- **Extending outwards to provide an outdoor balcony or terrace.**
  Depending on the configuration of your roof, you may be able to convert part of the loft into a living area and devote the rest to a roof garden.

A hinged fire-escape roof window gives onto a small roof terrace with timber flooring. Access is provided by a retractable ladder that is stowed in the bedroom cupboard when not in use. Take advice before you increase the load on an existing section of flat roof – for example, containerized plants can be very heavy.

An attic conversion has been turned into a children's playroom with plenty of floor space for games. Later on, the same space will earn its keep as a teen retreat. Adding sound insulation into the subfloor will prevent impact noise from becoming a nuisance on lower levels.

Building work

The work involved in converting a loft falls into two categories – structural and nonstructural. Changes to servicing will also be required – at the very least, extending electricity into the new space. You may need specialist advice from an architect or structural engineer to advise on the correct amount of strengthening that will be required for the roof and floor.

If you need to repair or renew your roof, it makes good financial sense to convert your attic at the same time, particularly if the conversion work would require the erection of up-and-over scaffolding, which forms a major part of the expense of both types of work. You may wish simply to carry out a basic conversion for the time being – install rooflights, strengthen and board out the floor – and postpone the installation of final finishes for later, when you actually need the extra room or have more funds.

Room for improvement: lofts can be fitted out to varying degrees of finish and habitability, depending on your circumstances, needs and available funds.

Structural work includes:

- Strengthening the joists to take the additional weight of fixtures and fittings, furniture and people. The joists in an attic are not as strong as floor joists elsewhere in the home, simply because they don't need to be. To convert an attic you need to ensure that the floor can bear the new weight, which generally entails 'doubling' up the joists by bolting on additional members alongside.
- Strengthening the rafters. Similarly, the roof structure is designed to carry the weight of the roof covering – and possibly a few inches of snow. For a loft to be used as a habitable room, rather than simply as a storage depot, you will need to install windows in the plane of the roof or construct a dormer. Windows are considerably heavy and to bear the extra weight the rafters will need to be strengthened by doubling up additional members alongside existing ones in the same way as the joists.
- If you are adding a dormer, you will need to provide some support for the roof structure over the new opening.

Nonstructural work will vary according to the level of finish you require and how you intend to use the space. It may include:

- Adding insulation between the joists and rafters.
- Cutting openings in the roof and fitting rooflights or constructing dormers.
- Widening the access hatch or building a staircase.
- Boarding out the floor to cover the joists and covering the rafters with plasterboard, wood, tongue-and-groove boarding or some other cover.
- Applying plaster or other finishes to exposed brickwork.
- Many lofts are where the cold-water cistern is located. For optimal layout of the new space, it might be necessary to move the cistern.
- Extending services, including electricity, heating and possibly water and drainage, to the loft.
- Extending soil stacks vertically above new roof windows.
- Fitting out the area under the eaves with built-in storage.
- Fitting out part of the area with bathroom fixtures.

Legalities

In many cases, converting an attic requires planning permission. In all cases, if you intend to live in the space in some sense, rather than just use it for storage, it will be subject to building control. Before embarking on any project, always seek advice on whether it is necessary to obtain permission.

- If you are going to be using the new space as a bedroom, office or other living area, it must have at least one window to count as a 'habitable' room. Bathrooms are exempt from this requirement, though they must be adequately ventilated by some form of mechanical extract; so if you want to convert a loft into an extra bathroom, it can be fully internal.

- Unless your home is listed or you live in a conservation area, you do not require planning permission to insert rooflights into the plane of your roof, because this type of change does not alter the roof shape or contour.

- Dormers at the rear are generally exempt from planning control, provided they are no greater than a specified size. Those at the front or the side, as well as those that look out over a public space, do require planning permission.

- If your attic conversion will increase the volume of your home by 15 per cent or more, it will require planning permission. That may well be the case if you live in a top-floor flat.

- Half the available floor space that results from the conversion must have a head height of 2.3m (7½ft) or more.

- Building control governs all structural work to the roof and floor of the new space. An inspector will have to approve the work before it is covered by boarding or final finishes.

- If the conversion work entails building onto party walls with neighbours, you will need to seek a party-wall award.

- In the case of homes that are over two storeys, not counting the attic, fire regulations come into play. A fire door or closed fire-protected stair may need to be installed to separate the new area from the rest of the house. The design and position of access stairs may also be governed by fire regulations, which can affect your options for layout.

Dormer windows increase the amount of floor area with adequate head height. This generous-sized attic conversion creates an elegant master suite, a perfect retreat from the rest of the house.

Types of window

There are as many types of roof windows as there are roof shapes and profiles. Specification can also vary considerably, with products at the higher end of the market incorporating all sorts of features, such as electric operation.

There are three basic types. Rooflights sit flush with the plane of the roof. Skylights also sit flush with the roof, but are usually unopenable. Dormer windows project from the roofline to increase floor area, are vertical and come in a variety of configurations.

Variations on the theme include:

- Centre-pivot windows, which have a control bar at the top so that you can operate the window from near head height. Furniture can be placed directly beneath, which allows you to make the most of available floor space. Centre-pivot windows also facilitate cleaning.
- Top-hung roof windows, which are opened using a handle at the bottom and are particularly suited to low-pitched roofs.
- Both centre-pivot and top-hung windows can be combined with additional vertical or sloping windows to increase the amount of daylight.
- Roof windows are also available that open out top and bottom to form a balcony or terrace.
- Special roof windows designed for listed buildings or conversions of traditional properties, including warehouses and barns, can be specified to blend discreetly with the existing roof.
- Escape or access roof windows open outwards or are hinged at the side and comply with means-of-escape regulations. These are useful for providing access to an adjoining terrace or external fire escape.

Other aspects to consider include:

- **Means of operation.** Windows can be opened with push bars (often spring-loaded), hand winders, pole winders (for high windows that are out of reach) and by electrical control.
- **Glazing.** Many roof windows have high-performance glazing, designed to provide a good level of sound and heat insulation. Safety and fire-rated glazing are also available, as is obscured glazing for bathrooms or other areas where you want additional privacy. Some glazing is coated to promote water run-off and reduce the need for cleaning.
- **Blinds.** Glare and heat gain can be a problem with high windows. There are many types of blinds suitable for roof windows on the market. Some windows incorporate blinds within the glazing unit.
- **Size and shape.** Many companies produce roof windows in a range of sizes and shapes. This allows the windows to be specified according to the dimensions of the existing roof structure and avoids the need to cut into rafters.

Types of roof window include top glazing, dormer windows projecting from the wall, and rooflights set into the plane of the roof.

Access

Organizing access to a converted loft needs careful thought. Most attics before conversion are accessed via a ceiling hatch, which may or may not incorporate a loft ladder of some description. Unless you intend to use the space simply as a storage area, you will need to improve upon that arrangement.

In nearly all cases, the hatch will need to be enlarged. This is not merely for ease of use, but also to allow larger items of furniture to be moved into the space. There is no point planning to use a loft as a bedroom if you find you are unable to move the bed up there.

At the same time, it is advisable to replace folding or retractable ladders with a fixed stair of some sort – a secured ladder, a spiral staircase or some other space-saving design, or a proper staircase. Which option you choose will, to a large extent, depend on how much room you have on the level below. Safety is also a consideration. If the new space will be in use every day, and especially if children or those who are not steady on their feet will be accessing it, you need to make sure that the stairs are secure and easy to negotiate.

Bear in mind that not all commercially available stairs meet building regulations with respect to pitch and height of risers. Always check with a building inspector that the design you are planning to use meets with approval. Nonslip treads are particularly useful if the stair is relatively steeply pitched. If your home is more than two storeys, any staircase will need to be enclosed and separated by a fire door.

Options include:
- **Sliding, retractable or folding loft ladders.** But these are suitable only if you are using the loft for storage. Heavy-duty loft ladders are available, typically in metal or wood.
- **Fixed ladders.** While these may be slightly more secure than a folding ladder, they can be difficult to negotiate and should not be relied upon in circumstances where you are going to be accessing the loft every day. A variation on this theme is the 'paddle' or 'monk's-steps' stairs, where the treads alternate.
- **Spiral stairs.** Turning in a curve or a series of angled steps around a central support, spiral stairs are space-saving, characterful and secure enough to function as a permanent means of access to a loft. In addition to heavy cast-iron examples (available in reproduction or from second-hand sources), there is a wide range of contemporary designs with treads in a number of materials, including wood, metal and glass. Spiral stairs are available to suit square or circular wells and in either clockwise or anticlockwise rotations.

- **Open stairs.** Stairs with open treads (that is to say, with no risers) are less visually intrusive than solid staircases. A related type is the stair with treads cantilevered from the wall.

- **Conventional stairs.** These take up the greatest amount of floor area and you may also lose space through turns and landings. However, a conventional staircase undoubtedly adds greatly to the convenience of accessing a loft and makes the space feel better integrated with the rest of your home.

ABOVE RIGHT
Spiral stairs are space-saving and secure enough to serve as a permanent means of access to a converted attic. There are many designs on the market; alternatively, spiral stairs can be custom-made in a range of different materials.

RIGHT
A sturdy ladder with its own handrail minimizes the loss of usable floor area on the level below.

Designing the layout

Converted lofts are often irregular in shape and you may need to juggle with the positioning of furniture and fittings to arrive at an optimum layout. Use a sketch plan (see page 23) and work it out on paper first.

ABOVE
Setting a bed with the headboard towards the eaves represents a good use of space where head height is limited. Low beds – essentially mattresses on the floor – are another option.

RIGHT
A bath has been inserted under the sloping plane of the roof. A vertical radiator serves as a heated towel rail, a space-saving feature in a restricted area.

The floor area where head height is greatest is obviously where you are going to be most comfortable standing and moving about. Under the eaves, where the roof slopes to the floor, is a good place for fitted storage. There may, however, be sufficient head height in front of a roof window for you to position a sink or a desk.

Think about low-level furniture if head height is particularly restricted. Low beds (or mattresses on low platforms), low tables and floor cushions can help to dispel any hint of claustrophobia.

How you will light the space should also be considered as early in the design process as possible, particularly if you are thinking of incorporating fixed or concealed forms of fitting. Central lighting should be avoided at all costs. It is unattractive and flat at the best of times, but in an attic it will cast deep shadows into the corners and make the space seem small, poky and confined. Instead, direct light upwards to enhance the sense of volume or wash the walls with directional light to create an ambient glow. The undersides of beams and rafters make unobtrusive locations for directional spotlights. Low-level lamps dotted around the room create overlapping pools of light and shade that can be very evocative. Remember to fit dimmer switches to the lighting controls, so that you can vary the light levels according to need and preference.

Surfaces and finishes

Unlike extensions, which generally need to be closely integrated, decoratively speaking, with the rest of your home, lofts are more self-contained, which means you can employ a contrasting style, if you want to, without setting up an awkward visual clash.

Think about the mood you want to create and how material choices can contribute to the overall atmosphere. If you're after a peaceful retreat from the bustle of the household, a pale or neutral decorative scheme that spreads the available light around strikes a note of calm purity.

ABOVE
A wall picked out in a warm orange shade adds an accent of colour without being too dominant.

RIGHT
Exposed brickwork gives a loft space depth of character and makes a striking contrast to smooth planes of white-painted new plaster.

Painted tongue-and-groove boarding makes a good alternative to plasterwork and has a countrified feel. Exposed brickwork and other natural materials add warmth and character to spaces that often feature odd angles and sloping planes. Vivid colour can be just as effective and help to underscore the intimacy of the space – or you could use it to pick out a single wall.

Decide whether you would like to call attention to any exposed beams or roof structure. If head height is relatively restricted in your loft space, it is probably best to lime, whitewash or paint these white – dark beams overhead can look rather oppressive. Otherwise you can finish them with a natural seal.

In practical terms, the two main aspects to consider are weight and sound insulation. Even a strengthened attic floor is not going to be robust enough to bear the weight of heavy floor materials such as stone and tile. And relatively hard surfaces, such as timber flooring in whatever format (plywood sheets, boarding or wood laminate), transfer impact sound, often at an uncomfortable level, to areas directly below, unless you install a subfloor that has sound-insulating properties. Remember that lofts do not usually suffer as much wear and tear as other areas in the home, as they do not see any through traffic, so floor coverings can be softer and less robust.

A minimal glass structure is supported by
glass beams for the ultimate in transparency.

Case study 4

Conversion of an attic in a period building

Many attics, particularly in Victorian terraced houses, provide a limited amount of usable floor space, welcome enough when space is tight, but usually not particularly generous. This attic in a period building, however, with its high beamed roof, is spacious enough to accommodate a suite of rooms, providing a serene, contemplative space away from the bustle of city life.

The owner, an artist, was looking for room both to work and relax in, and this sensitive conversion more than fulfils the brief. A dynamic feature of the layout is the central stair that rises in the middle of the workspace and provides a point of orientation for the bedroom at one end and the sitting area at the other. One wall of the staircase is hung with a collection of watercolour paintings, serving as a visual introduction to the studio space under the roof. The cool contemporary décor contrasts with the exposed old beams, reminders of the building's past and structure.

The access stair rises in the centre of that portion of the attic that is currently used as a studio. Matchboarding is painted a luminous pale blue, a colour inspired by the Dutch artist Vermeer's paintings of tranquil domestic interiors.

At one end of the converted space is a bedroom. The exposed beams form a strong unifying element running through all three connected areas, as does the sweep of wood flooring. Natural light comes from skylights set in the sloping plane of the roof.

The entire conversion provides 70 sq m (753 sq ft) of space. At the opposite end to the bedroom is a living room lit by skylights. Discreet uplighters mounted on the wall accentuate the spatial volume. If a building is listed, more substantial changes to roof shape, such as the installation of dormers, are usually not permitted.

Case study 5

**Loft conversion
providing master
bedroom and
en-suite bathroom**

With a growing family and
a live-in nanny, the clients
urgently needed a private
retreat. This attic conversion,
with its rooftop views,
provides them with a serene
space in which to escape
from the domestic hurly-burly.

At the front of the attic
windows are set into the plane
of the roof, while at the rear
a new dormer construction
maximizes floor area and
head height. The dormer was
made of acrylic sheeting and
features a generous horizontal
opening that is fitted with
'pan-optic' folding glass panels
so that it is possible to gaze
out over the London skyline.

Materials were deliberately
chosen to promote a truly
domestic, intimate feeling.
The stairs are left open to
allow light through to the
levels below. Most dramatic
of all is the shower ceiling
made of glass for starry
night-time views.

**Simple décor enhances the
feeling of intimacy. A rooflight
admits light at the front,
where any more elaborate
design would be refused by
the planners. Generous
storage is built in under the
eaves and where the plane
of the roof slopes down.**

LEFT
The view through the converted attic towards the en-suite bathroom.

BELOW LEFT
Wall-hung fixtures, such as lavatory, sink and radiator/ towel rail, maximize floor area in a tight space.

BELOW RIGHT
The shower is floored with simple pine decking. At the rear is a sheet of sandblasted glass dividing the shower from the new access stair: in this way, other family members always know when the shower is occupied. But the true show-stopper is the glass ceiling, for showers under the stars.

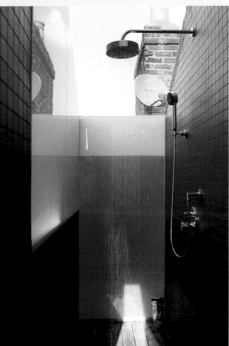

117

Case study 6

Converted top floor

When a couple bought the top two floors of a house in a conservation area, the top floor had not been used for years and was very dark with low ceilings. Yet planning restrictions prevented them from building upwards. Their dramatic solution was to raise the roof and replace it with glass. The new glazed roof framed in steel is controlled automatically and can be opened during fine weather or screened with a blind when the sun is too strong.

The pristine light-filled flat with its clever contemporary detailing belies the difficulties of the conversion work. Heavy items had to be craned into place very expensively; the rest of the building materials had to be hauled up three flights of communal stairs. The couple also decided to project-manage the scheme themselves, employing all the subcontractors directly, which exposed them to a number of headaches along the way. However, the bespoke result was well worth the wait and the effort.

ABOVE
The view of the new top floor with the glass roof slid back. Glass panels set into the floor of the upper level let natural light down to the floor below, so all parts of the flat benefit from filtered light. MDF was used for cupboard doors and walls that conceal storage, and also for doors through to hidden rooms.

RIGHT
The glass roof panels send light down into internal areas on the level below that would otherwise lack natural light.

The view of the top floor
looking through the dining
area towards the kitchen
at the far end of the space.
A ladder leading from the
kitchen counter provides
access to the roof terrace.
With the entire ceiling wide
open to the sky, changes in
the weather and the quality
of natural light throughout
the day animate the interior.

Until relatively recently, home improvements largely took place above ground. Loft conversions, extensions, new conservatories and changes to internal layout comprised the greater proportion of the major building works carried out on the domestic front. Nowadays, however, many homeowners are digging deep to find the space they need.

4 Basements

Digging deep

Britain is relatively unusual in that so few homes have full basements. Where basements do exist, they are often partial or consist of little more than coalholes, particularly in urban areas. That is not the case in many other parts of the world. In North America, for example, full-height basements are fairly standard in both new and old homes, and are typically used as family recreation rooms and for utility purposes.

Basement conversions have really taken off in the UK in the past ten years or so – for a number of reasons. One is sheer pressure of space. If you have already converted your loft or extended your home, don't want to move but need to increase your living area, the only option remaining may be to go underground. At a time when house prices are volatile, climbing one minute and sinking the next, it often makes financial sense to stay put, even though the costs of a basement conversion are higher than other forms of home improvement. But the real clincher is the fact that this type of conversion is much more feasible than it once was. New building materials and techniques, in particular new waterproofing systems, have proved extremely successful at controlling damp. The sensitive siting of lightwells, along with other strategies to introduce natural light into the new space, mean a converted basement can be light, dry and surprisingly airy – a far cry from the dark, musty, cobwebby glory hole of popular imagination. If your home doesn't already have a basement, even a partial one, the area under your home can still be excavated in the majority of cases, creating a whole new floor level.

The trend has recently been given a boost by government policy, which in turn has had an impact on the attitude of local authorities to these types of changes. New basements or basement conversions are viewed very favourably by the powers that be because they are environmentally friendly. They not only provide extra space without using up land – easing the pressure on green space – but they also reduce energy demands because, as earth-sheltered spaces, they absorb warmth from the ground. A house with a basement is estimated to be 10 per cent more energy efficient than a comparable house without one. Proposals are currently being put forward to encourage developers to include basements in new housing as a matter of course. For now, this shift in policy may help homeowners planning such projects to negotiate the approvals process more easily.

Converted basements can be light, airy and inviting, thanks to new building and waterproofing techniques – a welcome extension of living space.

Commissioning the work

Unlike other types of home conversion, where the package route is not necessarily the way to go, basement conversions are often best handled by specialist firms, a number of which have sprung up in recent years to take advantage of the increasing demand.

Many of these companies have imported materials and technology from Europe to deal with the particular challenges of creating a new living space underground. As with other specialist outfits, their services tend to include making feasibility studies, design and negotiating any official permissions, as well as carrying out the actual building work and the fitting out.

In major cities there may be a number of companies from which to make a selection. Away from national centres, however, your choice may be more limited. Always ask to see examples of previous work – you may even be given the option of visiting completed schemes, which can give you a much better idea of what a converted (or new) basement space will feel like, as well as suggesting possible design strategies. This part of the research process is important – most of us can imagine what a converted loft might look like but find it more difficult to get past our preconceptions about underground living.

This is not to say that you should do without an architect altogether. While specialist basement-conversion companies provide a design service, that expertise is generally directed towards coming up with a viable scheme for the basement itself. Where architects can excel is in conceiving a scheme as a whole, so that the new basement will be well integrated with the existing ground and upper levels. This often involves a degree of replanning and redesign over the entire home. Many architects who have experience in this area have also devised clever detailing that serves to enhance natural light in basement areas to an exceptional degree.

Excavating an area to the rear of your house to make a lightwell brings light into the basement.

Do your sums

Basement conversions and new basements are costly – there is no getting around that fact. How much you will need to spend will depend on a number of factors, including whether or not there is an existing basement (even a coalhole counts), the existing ground conditions (with special reference to the water table), the size of your home and the degree of finish you require.

New excavation costs more than enlarging or deepening an existing basement or cellar. There are also maintenance costs to consider. If you opt for a waterproofing system that includes a pump and sump, this plant should be checked over yearly and serviced as required.

Many experts advise that basement conversions become increasingly cost-effective the more your home is worth, so don't automatically expect to recoup whatever you spend on a conversion immediately – this type of project should not be viewed as a quick way of enhancing your property's value in the short term. At the same time, don't try to cut corners to save money in a way that could compromise the quality of the new space – that might even detract from the appeal of living areas on the ground level and above.

Many basement conversions are used for upmarket facilities, such as this home gym.

One option for basement lighting is top glazing. Part of the floor structure can be removed on the level above and fitted with strengthened flooring-grade glass.

Going underground

In spatial terms, basement conversions offer much more potential than one might expect. The most obvious is a direct increase in floor area. If you excavate and enlarge an existing basement, or dig out a new one, you will increase the size of your home by a full additional floor.

In theory, a basement can be dug down to two storeys, but in practice most conversions are single level only. However, compared with a loft conversion, where much usable floor area can be lost under the eaves, basements are potentially much more spacious. And, unlike with loft conversions, the problems associated with restricted head height do not apply. Most basement conversions provide a minimum of 2.4m (8ft) head height, some even more. There are also advantages when you compare basement conversions with more standard ground-level home extensions. Potentially contentious issues with neighbours, such as overlooking and loss of light, will not apply and you will not have to sacrifice very much of your garden – only what is needed to create lightwells or to provide separate access if that is required.

It is important to consider how you are going to use the new space, as that will affect the standard of finish and fitting out, and, consequently, the cost. There are few restrictions, nowadays, with respect to a basement's potential use, which means that kitchens and bathrooms can be sited underground. Many people find it difficult to shake off the basement's association with storage and general utility, but a considerable number of new underground spaces are now conceived as luxurious living areas complete with high-tech home cinema and games areas, or form a suite comprising master bedroom and bespoke bathroom. Others have been created to provide the kind of facilities one might expect of a day spa, such as a gymnasium, Jacuzzi and sauna. Particularly popular at the upper end of the market is the basement swimming pool. In addition, because they are potentially self-contained, basements also lend themselves to separate functions, serving as nanny or granny flats, home offices and the like.

At the same time, a relatively basic and small-scale basement conversion can do a great deal to ease pressure on the rest of your home. Enlarging and improving a cellar to serve as a utility area, for example, can allow you to move the freezer, boiler and laundry appliances below ground, freeing up additional room in your kitchen. And of course, there is always storage – no modern home can have too much of that.

Excavating a semi-basement into a space that provides full head height directly increases the floor area of your home by an entire level. With the extra room to play with, the layout of your entire home can be reconfigured.

GROUND CONDITIONS

A good basement-conversion company will be able to advise you on the feasibility of such a project. A key consideration is the existing ground conditions. It is often advisable to dig test holes at various locations around the exterior or perimeter of your home to determine both what type of foundations will be required and also the level of the water table. If the water-table level is too high, the cost of tanking or waterproofing the new basement may be prohibitive. Tree roots can also pose a problem. Another factor that can drive up cost is the presence of a solid ground-level floor slab, common in houses built after 1960. It is not impossible to dig out a basement under a concrete slab, but it adds to the difficulty and hence expense of the work.

Older Victorian and Edwardian properties, which typically feature small cellars or coal chutes under suspended timber floors, are easier to convert. In addition, most older houses have drains that are built to the side of the house, not underneath, which means the basement can be excavated to a depth of 3m (10ft), giving a space with full head height.

ABOVE
This converted basement benefits from a generous spill of light through a glazed end wall into an excavated lightwell in the rear garden.

LEFT
An open stairway and a translucent glass partition make the most of available natural light coming from the level above.

Permissions and other legalities

Most basement conversions require planning permission, particularly those that include a front lightwell. The size and style of lightwell can be contentious in some areas, particularly conservation areas, because the appearance of the front elevation will be affected. Some boroughs look more favourably on this type of alteration than others. Planning permission is also required if you intend to use the basement as a separate, self-contained area – as an office with its own street access, for instance, or as a separate flat.

ABOVE
A cheaper and less complex option is to excavate under an existing front or rear garden and install lightwells in the ground.

RIGHT
Existing shallow or semi-basements are easier to convert. Structural work includes providing new means of support and installing top glazing.

Converted basements that will be used as 'habitable' rooms will need to be inspected by the local building inspector and building regulations will apply with regard to fire protection, means of escape, drainage, and foundation design and construction, among other issues. It is important to comply to the letter – if the work is not passed on completion, you will not receive a Building Completion Certificate, which can make your home hard to sell in the future.

Another critical bureaucratic hurdle is the party-wall agreement. If your home forms part of a terrace or is semidetached, creating a new basement or enlarging an existing one will have an impact on neighbouring foundations. In such cases, neighbours are entitled to the services of a surveyor – which you must pay for – who will inspect the work to ensure that it has not impacted adversely on party walls. It is a good idea to involve your neighbours in your plans as early as possible to ease their minds about possible subsidence and forestall unnecessary objections.

Structural work

The construction work involved in converting a basement depends on what you've got in the first place. In most cases, structural alteration will be necessary, which means you will need the services of a structural engineer to calculate loadings and design new foundations.

Converting an existing basement with adequate head height is relatively simple. Stairs and access will need to be improved, new services routed to the area and openings created at ground level to draw down light. Damp-proofing will also have to be carried out before final finishes are installed. If your basement consists of a warren of small spaces, you will probably wish to remove dividing walls to create a single open area, and RSJs will need to be installed to support the ground floor.

Enlarging a partial basement or creating a new one is more complex. Because the entire load of a house – walls, floors and roof – is carried by its foundations, excavating underneath means underpinning. This used to be a messy and disruptive process, but new methods limit the disturbance as far as possible. These involve underpinning with concrete at intervals around the perimeter of the house prior to excavation. The basement is subsequently dug out through what will become the front lightwell. In theory, this technique means that the rest of the house remains quite habitable throughout the building works. In practice, some people find the resulting dust and noise make it preferable to decamp for a while. Creating a basement swimming pool necessitates double underpinning and excavating down to a depth of 5m (16ft) or so.

Basements do not have to be situated directly under the footprint of your house. Some people extend under their garden, which is a cheaper and less complex option that causes less disruption. In some cases, these garden warrens also have extensions built over the top.

DAMP-PROOFING
Basements, as underground areas, are naturally susceptible to water penetration. The traditional means of damp-proofing is tanking, which involves applying a waterproof coating over the walls and floor, which are themselves constructed of water-resistant materials. Tanking, however, is not infallible. As ground water rises, pressure can build up on walls and floors, particularly on the joints between them, causing movement and cracking through which water can penetrate.

The new approach to damp-proofing seeks to control and redirect water, rather than exclude it. This technique, employed by many basement-conversion firms, entails lining the walls and floor with cavity-drain membranes – sheets of plastic that direct water into channels and thence to a sump from which it is pumped into the main drains. The siting of sump and pump is arranged so that the plant can be readily accessed for yearly inspection and maintenance. Proprietary dry-lining systems are applied over the cavity-drain membranes.

The ultimate in underground luxury –
a basement swimming pool. Such features
obviously require even deeper excavation
than is needed for living spaces.

Light and air

What makes a basement truly habitable is light and air. The best and most sensitively designed basement conversions feel and look no different from spaces above ground – you'd be hard pressed to tell the difference.

Natural daylighting is a legal requirement for any habitable room, a stipulation that does not include kitchens or bathrooms, both of which can be fully internal. Ventilation is also a requirement to provide a healthy airflow. There are a number of ways by which such conditions can be met:

- Natural ventilation can be achieved through openable windows or through an open staircase connecting to the level above. If the basement is separated from the stairs by a door, or if it contains a kitchen, bathroom or bedroom and there are no openable windows, you will need to install an air pipe to draw in fresh air from the outside. A similar device is a sun pipe, a closed tube with a reflective lining that bounces light down into the basement.

- Lightwells are the most popular means of introducing light to underground spaces. There are a number of variations on the theme. The simplest is a window well set into the ground immediately next to the basement. This serves rather like a skylight; some designs can also be opened, which allows for natural ventilation. Larger lightwells necessitate excavating a shaft down to the basement floor level. The basement wall that borders the shaft is then fitted with a window, or floor-to-ceiling glazing or French doors, depending on site, context and other considerations. At ground level the lightwell may be covered with opaque toughened glass, a grille or pavement lights. If possible, fill the lightwell with greenery and planted pots so you don't look out onto a solid wall.

- Some existing basements have small openings that can be enlarged to raise light levels.

- If you extend the basement into the garden, you can provide access with French doors to create a sense of openness and light. Alternatively, you can install glazed panels in the basement ceiling to draw light down from above.

- Installing glazed panels in the ground floor directly above the basement is a good way of borrowing natural light.

- In extensive basements that are lit by one or more lightwells, consider replacing internal dividing walls with glass.

- Extending windows as high as they will go improves the quality of light. In some conversions, windows have been taken above ceiling height in a stepped detail to maximize natural light. The more sky that is visible, the more daylight a space will receive.

- Light, glossy surfaces and finishes make the most of available light.

In basement conversions extensive high-level glazing increases the amount of daylight that can enter the space in a dramatic fashion.

Access

Converting an existing basement or creating a new one involves providing a decent means of accessing the new space. Existing or partial basements are often reached by narrow stairs, which tend to be hidden behind a door on the ground floor. These may not be wide enough for everyday use or may be positioned awkwardly with regards to the layout of the new area.

If you intend to use the basement as an integral part of your existing home, open stairs descending from the ground level have many advantages. They do not impinge very much on the space below and they allow a free flow of light and air from above. Spiral stairs and stairs with open treads fall into this category.

Fire regulations or the need to keep the basement self-contained may dictate enclosed stairs. In this case, a door generally separates the stairs from the basement. External stairs can be used to connect a basement with the garden, which introduces a more dynamic quality.

ABOVE

Unless fire regulations dictate otherwise, open staircases from upper levels make a good means of access for basement conversions, as they allow more light through from above.

LEFT

Space-saving spiral stairs can be substituted for narrow, existing basement stairs without sacrificing any more usable floor area.

Case study 7

New basement

It's hard to believe, looking at the sunny airy kitchen of this London terraced house, but it was once a shallow basement void with sandy rubble for a floor. In its original state the house was typical of its kind, with front and back rooms on each floor. Instead of opening up the rooms in the type of conventional conversion that leaves two fireplaces exposed along one wall, the radical decision was taken to remove the floor of the ground-level back room altogether and dig deep to create the extra space and volume required.

A specialist company handled the excavation and structural work and although this was an expensive route, it paid off in the quality of the result. The contractors put in the necessary steelwork to support the back of the house and dug down 1.5m (5ft) and excavated another room's width to create space for the kitchen. The neighbouring property was underpinned and the new basement is fully tanked, with the floor slab drained underneath.

ABOVE
A particular feature of this conversion is the quality of natural light. Just beyond the kitchen island is a glazed bay window giving onto a lightwell excavated in the front garden that steps down in terraces. At the other end of the space light comes through the glazed wall and roof of the rear extension. The floor slab (finished in Spanish limestone) incorporates underfloor heating, the thermal mass meaning that the house is efficiently and evenly heated.

RIGHT

A small additional extension some 2.5m (8ft) square meant that the full width of the house could be glazed at the rear. With a glass roof over the top, this captures morning light. The small decked garden is a suntrap. The principal strategy of the conversion was to maximize the view from front to back and increase the apparent width through daylighting.

LEFT BELOW

Glass balustrading allows maximum light through. The basement receives natural light throughout the day.

LEFT

The island unit is made out of a carcase of standard kitchen units wrapped in stone, mitred at the edges to suggest greater depth. The flooring on the upper level and stairs is European oak – fitted by the client himself at weekends. Uplights set into the limestone kitchen floor create dramatic effects after dark.

Case study 8

Semi-basement renovation

When a couple traded in their open-plan loft for a Victorian terrace in need of some work, their priority was to re-create the big open spaces they were used to. A particular focus was the kitchen in the semi-basement, which was in a very dilapidated state.

The architect-designed solution was to rip out the kitchen, along with the shoddy conservatory attached to it, and excavate the garden further to provide room for a glazed extension. Because the house is part of a terrace, skiploads of earth had to be brought through the house. The single sheet of glass that forms the roof of the dining room extension was craned over the roof and lowered into position. The result – a single unified space that is flooded with light and reaches out into the patio – is used for entertaining and family life, and as a working area for one of the owners, who is a chef with his own catering company.

A view of the new basement extension with its glazed roof and glazed door to the garden. The old kitchen was stripped out and the area immediately adjacent excavated to make room for the extension.

The original kitchen was in a very poor state. Fully renovated, it now makes a seamless and efficient workspace for a professional cook. Both facing walls are fitted with units and worktops in a generous version of a galley kitchen. The lack of wall cupboards adds to the sense of space.

RIGHT

The dining area is located in the new extension of the semi-basement. A glass door separates it from the patio and slides back completely to draw the two spaces together. The glass roof is a particular attraction and draws light down into the interior.

Extensions come in all shapes, sizes and styles, from additions that blend so seamlessly with the original house that they look like they have always been there, to defiant contrasts that play with form and material in innovative ways. While the term 'extension' evokes a certain generosity of scale, in practice many extensions deliver enormous spatial benefits while taking up only a limited amount of ground area.

5 Add-ons

Branching out

Building an extension tends towards the more complex and expensive end of the home-improvement spectrum. You are almost certainly going to need professional design advice to come up with a workable scheme and get it past the necessary official hurdles, and you may well encounter a higher degree of resistance from neighbours and a more protracted planning process as a result. Exceptions include small extensions such as conservatories or glazed garden rooms, which generally do not require planning permission and can be erected without a great deal of difficulty, especially if they are made of prefabricated elements.

While a general sense that you are short of space may be the reason why you are considering an extension, it pays to be more specific in your plans from the outset. At the same time, keep an open mind as to how your needs might be best accommodated. As with other major building projects, an architect or design professional can help you to see the whole picture, so that you don't simply end up with extra floor area, but also improve the way your home works and feels overall. A particularly sensitive issue is how the new space will connect with the old – the size and scale of the opening, for example, or the way in which outdoor areas will subsequently be accessed.

ABOVE
Even relatively modest extensions, such as this addition to a kitchen at the rear of a property, can have a disproportionately large impact on existing living areas, in terms of both layout and quality of light.

RIGHT
A glazed pavilion, detailed in keeping with the existing architectural character of the house, creates an airy living space on an upper level.

Value for money

Adding value to your home is always desirable, even if you don't expect to move in the near future. Surveys reveal that the type of extensions most likely to increase sale value and the general desirability of a property are those that increase the size of the kitchen. The inclusive kitchen, which doubles as an informal living-eating area, is high on many people's wish lists when they go shopping for a new home. Conservatories have long been popular, while additional bathrooms are also welcome.

A well-planned and well-executed extension will add significant value to your home. This generous contemporary addition to a Victorian terraced house, with its steel framing infilled with sliding panels of glass, makes a bold contrast with the existing architecture. Serving as an open-plan kitchen, eating and living area, it also has the effect of merging the internal space with the garden.

If you live in a city, any extension that increases general living space will probably recoup its cost in terms of enhanced sale price. Other good investments include garages where cars can be kept securely off the street.

However, an extension can sometimes make your home a less desirable prospect, particularly if it has been badly designed and built. An extension that has simply been tacked onto your home, which carves up the garden or results in poor access is an undeniable eyesore. Less obviously, an extension that robs light from existing areas, renders their function redundant, or results in awkwardly shaped spaces and tortuous internal routes is simply money down the drain.

If possible, try to bracket the work of building an extension with any other improvements that need to be made to your home. This not only makes good financial sense, it is also less disruptive – you will only need to suffer the chaos of major works once.

Where to site the extension

When most people think about extending their homes, the obvious option is generally to the rear at ground level. This is not the only solution, however. If your garden is tiny or you don't want to sacrifice any of it, there may be other solutions open to you. Bear in mind that structural issues and planning guidelines will also have a bearing on what is feasible and what is not.

Another factor to consider is access. If you are planning to extend a terraced house without street access to the garden, plant and materials will have to be taken through the house, which can add greatly to the disruption and mess of the proceedings.

REAR EXTENSIONS AT GROUND LEVEL

By far the most common approach is to extend the house into the garden at ground level. Generally, rear extensions are less contentious in planning terms because they are screened from the street. Provided they do not increase your home by more than a certain amount (see page 156), they may not require permission at all. If you don't have a lot of garden space, you may be able to find the necessary area for an extension by demolishing existing outbuildings or utility areas, such as old pantries or sculleries, which are often tacked onto Victorian and Edwardian houses at ground level.

Building on at ground level to the rear offers the opportunity to extend living areas or kitchens, resulting in a more generous and light-filled space. Extensive glazing, sliding glass doors or French windows on the end or side walls will reinforce the link with outdoor areas, which can be further underscored by sympathetic choices of flooring indoors and out. You can also roof the extension in glass or construct it entirely of glass – the traditional conservatory is one option, but more contemporary designs are also effective, creating a warm, weather-tight room set amid the garden planting.

Rear extensions do not necessarily have to be single storey. A two-storey extension will cost twice as much as one that is single storey and will almost certainly need planning permission, but you may welcome the additional space and the chance to integrate the extension on both ground and first-floor levels. What might supply an extended kitchen-diner on the ground floor, for example, could provide an additional bathroom, home office or bedroom on the first floor.

Planning officers are less likely to object to contemporary additions if they are at the rear of the property. Here the opportunity has been taken to create a two-storey extension, substantially increasing the floor area.

SIDE EXTENSIONS

Often overlooked, particularly in urban areas where housing tends to be dense, side extensions can be very effective. If you live in a detached house with plenty of surrounding land, side extensions may appear to offer more immediate potential, but this option can also deliver surprising benefits where space is tight.

In urban areas there is often a narrow strip of land separating one property from another. In most cases, this 'side return' is paved and serves to give access from the street to the garden at the rear of the house. Rarely of much use for planting, the side return can be absorbed into the ground floor of your home to create a more generous kitchen or living area. Glazing the roof of the side extension will give a better quality of natural light. Because you are building up to the property line with your neighbour, you will need to obtain planning permission and a party-wall award. Some exceptionally cooperative neighbours have undertaken such projects jointly, extending their homes to either side of the boundary wall.

LEFT AND ABOVE

This extension absorbs the formerly redundant side return between a terraced house and its neighbouring property. Annexed to the ground-floor living area, the side return provides room for a kitchen to be arranged down its length, the entire structure lit by a sloping glass roof.

ROOF EXTENSIONS

Many homes have existing ground-floor extensions or staggered levels where bathrooms, for example, are accessed off half-landings. In some cases, these can provide a site for an additional extension built over the top. Adding an extra storey to the top of your home is another possibility, though in conservation areas or in areas where all the houses are the same height, this is unlikely to gain approval. Top-level extensions not only add a whole new storey to your home, they also offer the possibility for top lighting, which can introduce a more dynamic quality to existing internal areas. An alternative is to add a single room onto the top of your roof and turn the remainder of the space into an outdoor terrace or roof garden.

LEFT AND ABOVE
Light floods through the glazed trussed roof of this add-on to a lower-level extension. Folding doors open up the space to a high-level terrace.

155

Planning permission and other legalities

An extension will have a greater impact on neighbours and the immediate environment than internal changes such as basement and loft conversions. Some extensions are exempt from planning, but many are not. Your local planning office should be your first port of call to find out whether your plans need approval or not.

Be prepared for delay. Changes are now being proposed to speed up the process, which can be unnecessarily protracted through a sheer backlog of cases – more than 50 per cent of the average council's planning caseload is made up of domestic applications and nearly nine in ten of these are eventually approved.

Under current guidelines you will **not** require planning permission for an extension if it is less than a certain size and conforms to other conditions:

- In the case of a terraced house or a house in a conservation area, the extension should be no more than 50 cubic metres (1,765 cubic feet) or represent more than 10 per cent of the original house volume, whichever is the greater.
- For other houses, detached or semidetached, that figure is 70 cubic metres (2,472 cubic feet), or 15 per cent of the original house volume.
- Size is calculated from external measurements, not internal floor area.
- The upper limit is 115 cubic metres (4,061 cubic feet).
- The definition of 'original house volume' excludes any extension built since 1 October 1973. 'Extensions' are also deemed to include garages and garden buildings within 5m (16ft) of the proposed extension.
- Design and materials must conform with the original house.
- No part of the extension should be nearer to any road than the part of the original house nearest the road.
- The extension must not be higher than the existing house, or higher than 4m (13ft) if it comes within 3m (10ft) of the property boundary.
- The extension and any other buildings on the property (excluding the original house) must not take up more than half the area.
- The extension is not being made to a listed building.

In the case of extensions that do require planning permission or those that back onto a party wall (which require a party-wall award), it is important to involve your neighbours as early in the planning process as possible. Talk the scheme over with them, explain what you are proposing to do and give them advance warning as to when the building works are likely to begin and for how long they are likely to last – demolition, site preparation, deliveries and construction work are often noisy, messy and disruptive for neighbours as well as yourself. Try to take into account any reasonable objections to your plans before you submit the scheme for approval. Schemes that are turned down tend to be those that block natural light from neighbouring properties, so roof pitches can be critical. As with any other conversion work that involves building onto party walls, you will have to pay for your neighbours to hire a surveyor to ensure that your extension will not affect the structural integrity of their homes.

Whether or not the extension requires planning permission, it must conform to building regulations, which means the works will have to be inspected at key stages (as outlined in Sequence of work, pages 38–9). The laying of foundations and drains and the construction of the main structure are key inspection stages. Building codes are constantly updated, particularly in the general area of energy-efficiency. Any extension will need to conform with the latest standards of insulation and energy-efficient lighting, whether the rest of your home does or not. Similarly, extensions must also comply with fire regulations and other health and safety guidelines.

ABOVE RIGHT
At the sacrifice of a small amount of garden space a single-storey extension opens up the back of the house. What is lost at ground level is made up for by the new terrace on the roof of the extension.

RIGHT
An airy steel framework extends out into the garden, creating an intermediate zone between the house and garden.

What's involved

One of the reasons why building an extension is generally more complex than other types of home conversion is that it always requires structural work. This often means that you will need to employ a structural engineer to calculate the type of foundations required or the size of structural elements such as concrete lintels or RSJs.

Building work includes:

- Laying new foundations – in the case of rear and side extensions – and tying them into existing foundations. If you are planning an extension over an existing extension or on top of your roof, you will need to seek advice as to whether the existing foundations need to be strengthened – by underpinning, for example.
- Possible rerouting of drains or extension of drains. All changes to drainage must be inspected.
- Erection of the shell and roofing, followed by the fitting out.
- Extension of servicing to the new area.
- Creating an opening in an existing external wall to provide access to the new extension. This generally entails installing a beam or joist over the opening to compensate for the loss of a section of load-bearing wall.
- If you are extending on top of your roof, you will need to install stairs or some other means of access to the new level.

RIGHT
Specifying, detailing and constructing such minimal glass structures is a job for the professionals. When you are planning to use expanses of glass, it is often advisable to specify toughened glass for safety and security. Low-E glass, which helps to prevent excessive heat loss, is another option.

OVERLEAF
A particular benefit of a new extension is the opportunity it provides to introduce windows and openings on more than two sides. A typical terraced house is lit by windows at the front and rear; windows to the side or above create a more dynamic play of light.

Conservatories and other prefab solutions

Adding a conservatory or glazed garden room has long been a hugely popular home improvement – for a nation of garden lovers where the weather can be unpredictable, a conservatory brings us close to the garden without exposing us to the elements. Most designs are traditional in style, can be erected very quickly after the foundation slab is laid, and represent a relatively economical and simple solution if that is the type of extension you prefer.

Other companies produce prefab or kit extensions that are tailored more to individual specification. These can be produced to match the style of your home; some even come ready-made from the factory and are craned into position. Once servicing is extended to the new area, they are fully habitable.

A wide range of companies produce off-the-shelf conservatories. The most common styles are Victorian, Edwardian and Georgian, though sun lounges and lean-tos are also popular. Most feature uPVC frames, though hardwood and aluminium frames are also available; roofs can be either flat or steepled.

Some companies will not only supply the basic kit of parts, but will also erect the conservatory for you. If you decide not to opt for this inclusive package, you will need the services of a builder to lay the foundations and erect what is known as a 'dwarf' wall on which the glazing rests (though some conservatories are glazed down to the ground and do not require dwarf walls). Foundations have to be perfectly level and fit the conservatory precisely – it is not a job for an amateur. Complications can arise if the position of the conservatory means that you need to build over drains or move a manhole.

The smaller conservatory designs are generally exempt from planning permission, unless you have already extended your home or unless your house is listed or in a conservation area. They are also exempt from building regulations, provided they meet the following conditions:

- The roof is transparent or translucent.
- The floor area is less than 30 square metres (323 square feet).
- Glazing is toughened safety glass, which fractures into harmless pebbles.
- There is no drainage in the conservatory (for example, for a sink or lavatory).

An elegant conservatory traditionally styled serves as a dining room. Additional seating is arranged on the decking immediately outside, making a great space for entertaining.

CLIMATE CONTROL

All that transparency comes at a cost – which can be uncomfortable heat gain in summer and heat loss in winter. Unless you want to roast or freeze, depending on the season, you will need to ensure that you keep internal temperatures within a temperate range. This can be achieved in a variety of ways:

- Think about the possibility of installing radiators or underfloor heating if your conservatory faces north or east and is therefore likely to be cool.

- Low-E glass is a good insulating option. It has a special coating that reflects heat back into the interior. Alternatively – and expensively – you could opt for double glazing.
- Vents and openable windows allow a cooling airflow when the weather is warm. Roof and side window blinds also cut down on glare.
- Roof skylights are available that open or close automatically according to ambient temperature. These may be controlled either electronically or mechanically.

LEFT AND ABOVE
This sliding glazed construction is neatly integrated to the rear of the house and can be slid back when weather permits.

Material character

The materials you choose to construct your extension – to clad it and to form its structure – will have a dominating effect on its appearance. Extensions are highly visible, which is why they attract such close scrutiny from planners.

The least contentious approach to the design of an extension is to replicate the style of the original house as far as possible. If your home is listed or in a conservation area (and the extension will be visible from the street), you may be forced to follow this approach to win approval. However, matching detailing and materials is not necessarily straightforward. To achieve a visually acceptable result, you will have to go to a degree of trouble – sourcing bricks of the right colour and size, for example, if your home is brick-built – matching the size, scale and detailing of windows and other openings, and choosing appropriate roof finishes. You may wish to source elements from second-hand outlets such as architectural salvage yards. Old bricks, for instance, tend to blend in better than new ones that have not yet weathered, but they may be more expensive.

At the opposite end of the design spectrum are home extensions that are specifically designed to make a bold contrast to the existing architecture. In most cases, that difference is a function of the structure itself rather than more superficial treatments in terms of the cladding and detailing.

Lightweight steel structures allow walls to be mere infills of glass, a degree of transparency that can be very welcome when you are extending out into the garden. Timber-frame structures are another option. Not so long ago, timber-frame building was viewed askance by planners because of the perceived fire risk. These days it is looked upon much more favourably and is becoming increasingly common. The advantages of timber-frame building are cost, environmental friendliness and speed. You may be able to source prefab structural elements that will allow the construction to proceed faster than it would if you were building in brick and block. Timber-frame structures also lend themselves to insulating with eco-friendly materials, such as recycled newspaper, and generally work out cheaper than bespoke steel frames.

If you decide to opt for an extension that makes a defiant contrast in terms of style and architectural character to the rest of your house, you may have more of a battle on your hands with the planning department. Not all planners are conservative in their outlook, however. Pay a visit to the local planning office at an early stage to see if your approach is likely to be welcomed.

A shallow timber-framed glazed box at the rear of a terraced house accommodates a stairway, creating more floor space internally and bringing in more light.

Whichever approach you choose, the important thing is to be wholehearted. Extensions that are well built and well designed, whatever their style, merit approval. Don't be tempted to cut corners in the interests of economy, or you may well detract from the value of your home.

GLASS HOUSES

One of the great advantages of building an extension is the opportunity it provides to improve levels of natural light indoors. Increasingly, many side and rear extensions are built entirely of glass, transparent light boxes that will banish any tendency to winter blues. Such structures can be minimally detailed with the sheets of glass supported on brackets and glazed roofs carried by transparent glass beams. Other framing choices include steel, for a crisp contemporary look, or green oak, which has more of a rustic appearance. Doors that slide back or fold away reinforce the connection with outdoor areas. In the same way, making sure that the flooring indoors is level with decking or paving outside creates a seamless transition between indoors and out.

ABOVE
A bold glass box framed in white-painted steel is a modern interpretation of a perennial favourite.

LEFT
The simplicity of this metal-framed glazed garden room works well with the rough stone walls of a country cottage.

Garages, sheds and other outbuildings

For many people, the search for extra room takes them up the garden path. Utilitarian structures such as garages, sheds and other outbuildings can be converted or erected to provide a welcome annexe of living or working space. With the right approach, these can be surprisingly stylish and full of character. For the freelancer working from home, an outbuilding of this kind makes an excellent office with the necessary psychological separation from the rest of the household.

LEGALITIES AND OTHER PERMISSIONS

Small freestanding structures such as sheds pass beneath most people's radar when it comes to thinking about usable floor area. But in planning law sheds, garages and other outbuildings may be considered as 'extensions', depending on their size and location.

Whether or not you will require planning permission for this type of conversion depends on a number of factors. If you are converting a garage that is either attached to your home or freestanding and you have not already used up your 'permitted development rights' on other extensions – that is, if the resulting volume falls within the prescribed limits (see page 156) – you probably won't need planning permission, unless you are intending to carry out major changes that would affect the appearance of your home from the street, your home is listed or you live in a conservation area.

Small sheds and outbuildings (those less than 10 cubic metres/353 cubic feet) are not treated as extensions, but their presence reduces the allowance for further development. Large sheds (those more than 10 cubic metres/535 cubic feet) are treated as extensions if they are sited within 5m (16ft) of the existing house. You may also need planning permission if you live in a conservation area or you are not the sole freeholder of your property.

Err on the side of caution and investigate the position with your local planning officer first. If you intend to buy a prefabricated shed from a company specializing in upmarket outbuildings, make sure that the company agrees in writing to refund your deposit should planning permission be refused. Otherwise you could end up owning an expensive shed with nowhere to put it.

General rules include:
- The structure must not take up more than half of your garden.
- It must be sited behind the building line.
- It should be a given distance from the boundary (requirements vary).
- It should be less than 4m (13ft) high if it has a ridged roof, or 3m (10ft) high otherwise.
- It should be a given distance from a main road (requirements vary).

Small freestanding structures such as this chalet-style shed can be put to all sorts of uses, providing an extra living area, guest annexe or home workspace.

Even if planning permission is not required for your conversion, it makes sense to tell your neighbours about your plans. It is far better to ensure they are happy about what you are proposing to do before the event than find they are hopping mad once the structure has gone up.

Another possible area of contention may arise if you intend to use the new space for commercial purposes. As a study or home office, it will be exempt from restrictions (even if you earn your living there), but a structure that serves as a business premises will not. If, for instance, you are intending to convert a barn or other type of outbuilding to house a new commercial activity, your plans will fall under legislation concerning 'change of use'. In some areas councils may welcome the employment generation that such schemes provide; in others the impact on neighbours, in terms of increased traffic as a result of deliveries, visiting customers or clients, may count against you.

Converted nondomestic properties must also conform to the other regulations that govern building work – health and safety, fire regulations, means of escape and so on. Prefabricated 'home office' sheds are generally supplied insulated; if you are converting an attached or detached garage to serve as living quarters, you will need to bring the insulation up to current standards.

ABOVE AND LEFT
In one of the more unusual conversions of domestic outbuildings, this Second World War bomb shelter half-sunk into the garden has been turned into a sauna and shower.

Converting outbuildings

Attached garages can be absorbed very easily into the rest of your home simply by adding a connecting door between the two if one does not already exist. It is also a relatively simple procedure to install windows in place of the existing garage doors. The opening is already made, so you won't be affecting the structure of your home.

Because most attached or integral garages face the street, you may need to obtain planning permission for this type of conversion. You are more likely to gain approval if the style of the new windows is in keeping with those at the front of your house. If your garage is single storey, installing top lighting in the form of rooflights might be another option. Otherwise, the work largely consists of fitting out the interior, adding insulation and extending central heating and other services if these do not already exist.

Detached garages, substantial sheds or other robust outbuildings can also be converted as stand-alone extensions. You may wish to integrate these more closely with your house by building a covered walkway, for example, to give you some protection from the elements in bad weather. Such annexes often make good places for home offices, studios or guest accommodation, being at one remove from the rest of the household.

One major issue is the need for natural daylighting. By law all habitable rooms must have at least one window, but some nondomestic buildings, particularly old agricultural buildings, may lack windows altogether. Putting in new windows can be contentious in planning terms if the building is listed or within a conservation area. Of course, this also entails structural work because you will be making changes to either load-bearing external walls or the roof structure.

Top lighting, via rooflights or skylights, can be an effective and unobtrusive way of bringing natural daylight down into interior spaces, particularly if there are neighbouring properties close by. Companies that specialize in what are known as 'conservation windows' can be a good source for designs that are more likely to win approval. Conservation rooflights, for example, have slim profiles so they sit really flush with the roof, and are modelled on cast-iron framed Victorian examples.

A mews that once might have served as a garage – or previously stabling – has been turned into a compact modern townhouse. Siting the bedroom at the lower level where the quality of natural light is not so critical allows living areas to be arranged above.

Elsewhere, the detailing, framing and positioning of windows should be designed with careful attention to the period of the property and its former use. Installing standard off-the-shelf windows in a converted barn would be incongruous, to say the least. A sash window, for instance, takes its proportions and scale from the elevation of a typical Georgian or Victorian house and would be wildly out of place in a barn dating from a similar period. What often works better is to infill existing openings – such as overscaled doors – with glazing. This robust approach is a much more sympathetic way of responding to a structure that is generally rugged and plain.

Otherwise, the conversion work consists basically of fitting out and extending services. You will need to add insulation to increase energy-efficiency and make the space more comfortable, as well as upgrade floors and wall coverings. Running an electricity supply out to a garden structure means sinking cabling underground where it cannot be disturbed either by animals or by human digging activity. Always hire a qualified electrician to carry out such work.

ABOVE
Exposing the structural framework allows the quality of the original building to shine through.

LEFT
Robust agricultural buildings have great strength of character that needs to be matched in the detailing of any conversion. Industrial-style windows are a better bet than those more commonly used domestically.

177

New outbuildings

If you are considering expanding your floor area by installing a shed in the garden, an increasingly popular option is to buy a prefabricated structure from one of the upmarket companies that produce designs specifically intended to be used as additional living space or home offices. A far cry from the creosoted utility sheds for housing mowers and garden tools, these range stylistically from rustic cabins and cheery beach huts to smart chalets and mini clapboard houses complete with porches.

While 'luxury' sheds don't come cheap, even a small shed can add up to 5 per cent to a property's value. Any activity that might benefit from a little separation from the rest of the household can be usefully accommodated in these stand-alone structures, whether it is working from home, putting up overnight guests or giving your teenagers somewhere to make their own special brand of havoc.

Be aware that such off-the-shelf solutions are not necessarily that speedy. You will need planning permission for larger sheds, which can take a couple of months. In addition, concrete slabs have to be laid to serve as foundations and the shed itself will need to be fabricated and delivered. While the structure, once it has been delivered to the site, will be up and fitted out in a matter of days, the entire project may take as long as six months.

Don't commit yourself to a purchase solely on the basis of a glossy brochure or fancy website. It is important to visit the showroom to get an idea of what the shed looks like in reality and what the interior spatial quality feels like. Some companies allow customization – for instance, if the shed feels a little dark or confined, you might consider asking for a rooflight to be added. Ask to see examples of previous projects and make sure that the company is a bona fide operation – in other words, take the same precautions as you would if you were hiring a building firm. After all, it is a substantial investment.

ABOVE AND RIGHT
New outbuildings are widely available off the shelf in kit form, many specifically designed to serve as home offices or studios.

Even a prefabricated or kit-of-parts shed needs to be got into your back garden somehow. Access is a key issue. Some companies will crane a ready-made shed into position; others need to be satisfied (with photographic evidence) that access of some kind is possible and there aren't insuperable obstacles to delivery. If the company can't deliver your shed, you may have to pay a penalty.

Planning regulations may dictate where your shed can be sited. Other aspects to consider include:

- **Which part of your garden gets the sun**. If you are going to be working in your shed, you may wish to site it in a shady spot so the interior does not heat up uncomfortably.
- **Distance from the house**. If you have a very large garden, don't be tempted to site your shed in a really remote location. In bad weather you might be less keen to venture down a muddy path to reach it.
- **Servicing**. You may not need a water supply – a water cooler can provide you with cool drinks or water for making tea – but you will need power for lighting, radiators and fans. If you need to use a computer, check whether you can run it wirelessly from the shed, hooking into your home network. Similarly, you may not need a landline for a phone – just a mobile.

- **Security**. Site the shed where it is not too obscured by trees or greenery and thus more tempting to burgle, keep as few valuables as possible in it overnight and consider fitting a security system.
- **Maintenance**. If you are going to need to treat the structure regularly – repaint it, for example – make sure that you have easy access on all sides.

Before the shed is delivered, either complete or in prefabricated elements, the site must be prepared, cleared of vegetation and laid in concrete. This is a job for a professional. The base must be perfectly level and of the right depth to support the weight of the structure without ground movement or subsidence. Concrete does not dry immediately but needs a couple of months, depending on the weather, to 'cure' or fully harden.

A room with a view – a small geodesic dome, reminiscent of the structures created by Buckminster Fuller, provides an all-weather seating area at the end of a garden.

Add-ons   New outbuildings

181

Case study 9

Glazed side return

The side return, or narrow strip of land that typically sits between the side walls of adjacent terraced houses, can provide a much more promising site for extension than it might at first seem. Unlike rear gardens, side returns are generally not much use for planting and are often paved. Enclosing this side return and absorbing it into the kitchen made a dramatic improvement to the quality of the existing space and provided room for an eating area.

Advances in glass technology mean that glass boxes no longer need to overheat in summer or lose heat in winter. Various types of high-performance glass can be used for interior climate control and saving energy. In addition, very strong triple-laminated glass means that glass can now play a structural role in the form of glass beams that provide ultimate transparency.

The delicate transparency of the glazed wall and roof belies their strength: the laminated glass beams mean there is minimal interruption to light. The exposed brick walls make a rugged contrast to the pavilion-like extension. At night, uplighters set into the pale stone floor produce dramatic lighting effects.

LEFT
The glazed extension opens directly onto a paved terrace, extending the house into the garden. The glazed door is steel-framed.

LEFT AND ABOVE
The extension transformed a narrow poky area into an inclusive kitchen and eating space. The new kitchen is compactly laid out along one wall, with high-level cupboards for storage and further built-in storage to the left of the trolley. Pale stone flooring unites the kitchen and new extension. Along with the white units and walls, it makes the most of the natural light spilling in through the glazing.

183

Case study 10

Converted garage

From the outside it's an average garage; from the inside it's a light and airy space that provides much-needed extra room. Garage conversions can be fairly straightforward, but whether they represent value for money depends on where you live. In densely populated areas where off-street parking is at a premium, houses with garages can be highly sought-after. If there are alternative parking arrangements, however, the extra habitable space should enhance the value of your home.

In this case, the clients needed more living space to accommodate their growing family. The planners agreed to the scheme they proposed provided that the extension still looked like a garage from the street.

Some garages can be directly converted. Here the original 1970s structure was unsuitable and none of it remains. Instead, the garage doors open onto a 2m- (6ft-) deep storage space for bicycles and the like. The rest of the extension is accessed from the main house and serves as a playroom and occasional dining room.

From the street the new extension looks exactly like a garage. The planners stipulated certain elements of the façade detailing, requesting that the mouldings on the house and extension line up. The garage doors do not provide access to the new living area, merely to a small storage and servicing space.

BELOW
Sliding doors provide access from the main house into the new extension. Although most of the time the space is used as a playroom, it is sometimes used for entertaining.

LEFT
A generously scaled window at the rear of the building draws in plenty of natural light and provides views of the garden. Although the main house had enough bedrooms, the family were short of living space, particularly a place where children could spread out their toys and play.

ABOVE
Carrying through the same decoration from the main house into the extension results in a seamless flow of space. White walls and wooden flooring unite the living room with the adjacent play area. Simple storage drawers absorb the clutter. The sliding door allows the playroom to be closed off when it is not in use.

Case study 11

New extension

Built on the site of a former garage, this new extension provides room for a double-height kitchen and eating area. The exterior of the extension was designed to reflect the structural form of local barns; with its western red cedar and iroko cladding, it is also in keeping with the adjoining timber-framed cottage. The architect was keen to keep the new structure more reticent than typical barn conversions, so the sliding timber-framed glazed door that leads onto the veranda is subtly proportioned and detailed.

Internally, the new kitchen and eating area is a blend of classic and contemporary style. Materials are robust, economic and muted in tone, with off-white walls and unit fronts, blocked oak worktops and a floor made of concrete slabs that do a very good job of imitating flagstones. Tongue-and-groove units proved too expensive, so MDF routed with V-grooves was used for a similar effect. The soaring height is accentuated by well-judged lighting: wall-mounted uplighters, transparent pendants and concealed task lighting.

The double-height kitchen and eating area in a new extension on the site of a former garage provides an airy and expansive space with a good quality of natural light. The kitchen it replaced was dark, isolated and poky. The dining table and Welsh dresser were brought out of storage to furnish the new area – there wasn't room for them before.

RIGHT
From the exterior the form of the extension echoes the structure of local barns. Timber cladding will weather with exposure to a greyish tone. The deep overhang creates a sheltered veranda. The siting of the extension blends in perfectly with the existing garden.

FAR LEFT
One particular success in terms of materials is the floor made of concrete slabs finished to resemble flagstones. The product is normally used externally but looks surprisingly authentic.

LEFT
The generous opening that connects the new space to the veranda is infilled with sliding glass doors framed in timber, which is less visually obtrusive from the exterior than uninterrupted glazing would be.

Resources

Architect's Registration Board (ARB)

www.arb.org.uk
email: info@arb.org.uk
Tel: 020 7580 5861
Useful for an up-to-date register of architects

Architecture & Surveying Institute

www.ciob.org.uk
email: reception@ciob.org.uk
Tel: 01344 630700
Provides information on how to find a builder

The Association of Plumbing and Heating Contractors (APHC)

www.competentpersonsscheme.
  co.uk
email: aphc.uk@aol.com
Tel: 02476 470626
Through the 'Find A Plumber' search facility you will be able to locate the APHC licensed plumbers who are nearest to you

Council of Registered Gas Installers (CORGI)

www.trustcorgi.com
email: enquiries@trustcorgi.com
Tel: 0870 401 2300
Allows you to carry out searches for accredited professional installers near you

Electrical Contractors Association (ECA)

www.eca.co.uk
email: electricalcontractors@
  eca.co.uk
Tel: 020 7313 4800
You can find an ECA member using the website's search engine

The Federation of Master Builders (FMB)

www.fmb.org.uk
Tel: 020 7242 7583
Website includes a link to www.findabuilder.co.uk, through which you will be able to locate an accredited professional in your area

Fenestration Self Assessment Scheme (FENSA)

www.fensa.co.uk
email: enquiries@fensa.org.uk
Tel: 0870 780 2028
Trade association for those who install windows and doors in homes. Supplies information to the general public about FENSA registered organizations

The Institute of Plumbing and Heating Engineering

www.iphe.org.uk
email: info@iphe.org.uk
Tel: 01708 472791
By typing your postcode into the website's 'Find a Plumber' search engine, you will be able to locate an accredited professional in your area

Institution of Structural Engineers (IstructE)

www.istructe.org.uk
Tel: 020 7235 4535
Search for accredited professionals through Findanengineer.com

National Federation of Builders

www.builders.org.uk/nfb
email: nfbnat@builders.org.uk
Tel: 020 7608 5150
Website contains information on finding a builder for home improvements and conversions

National Federation of Roofing Contractors

www.nfrc.co.uk
email: info@nfrc.co.uk
Tel: 020 7436-0387
Search facilities on the website allow you to locate members in your area

National Home Builders Council (NHBC)

www.nhbc.co.uk
Tel: 01494 735363
Offers warranties on conversions but only if they are done by a professional builder on the NHBC register

National Home Improvement Council

www.nhic.org.uk/Pages
email: info@nhic.org.uk
Tel: 020 7828 8230
The website provides a list of NHIC members and organizations. Also provides ideas and advice on a range of improvement and maintenance options

The Royal Institute of British Architects (RIBA)

www.riba.org
email: info@inst.riba.org
Tel: 020 7580 5533
30,000 strong membership. Website helps you search for architects based on the kind of work you are doing

Royal Institute of Chartered Surveyors (RICS)

www.rics.org.uk
email: contactrics@rics.org
Tel: 0870 333 1600
Website allows you to search for accredited professionals and firms in your area

CONSERVATION SOCIETIES

About Listed Buildings
www.heritage.co.uk
Information and advice regarding listed buildings

CADW
www.cadw.wales.gov.uk
The official guardian for the built heritage of Wales

English Heritage
www.english-heritage.org.uk
email: customers@english-heritage.org.uk
Tel: 0870 333 1181
Website provides information on appropriate procedure for those interested in converting listed buildings

Historic Scotland
www.historic-scotland.gov.uk
email: hs.inspectorate@scotland.gsi.gov.uk
Tel: 0131 668 8701/8705
Conservation advice for homeowners and information about listed building consent

Society for the Protection of Ancient Buildings (SPAB)
www.spab.org.uk
email: info@spab.org.uk
Tel: 020 7377 1644
Information about conservation and period buildings

GOVERNMENTAL AND ENVIRONMENTAL ORGANIZATIONS

Association of Environmentally Conscious Building
www.aecb.net
email: graigoffice@aecb.net
Tel: 0845 4569773
Advice on sustainable building and environmentally friendly procedure. The website also contains useful search facilities

Centre for Alternative Technology (CAT)
www.cat.org.uk
Tel: 01654 705950
Advice on environmental issues

Commission for Architecture and the Built Environment (CABE)
www.cabe.org.uk
Tel: 0207070 6700
Advice on well-designed housing

Department for Communities and Local Government (DCLG)
www.communities.gov.uk
Tel: 020 7944 4400
Information on a range of housing issues

Energy Saving Trust
www.est.org.uk
Tel: 0800 512 012
Website contains plenty of information about being energy-efficient in your home

PLANNING

Planning-Applications
www.planning-applications.co.uk
email: where@planning-applications.co.uk
Online planning aid

The Planning Inspectorate
www.planning-inspectorate.gov.uk
email: enquiries@planning-inspectorate.gsi.gov.uk
Tel (England & Scotland): 0117 372 6372
Tel (Wales): 029 2082 3866
Information on a range of planning issues, such as obtaining planning permission for listed buildings

Planning Portal
www.planningportal.gov.uk
The government's online planning and building regulations resource includes facilities for online applications for planning permission

Plans Drawn
www.plans-drawn.co.uk
Provides drawings for planning permission applications to the local authority as well as information on requirements

rebuild
www.ebuild.co.uk
Information on planning permission

UK Planning
www.ukplanning.com
Information and resources about planning provided by participating local authorities

BUILDING AND OTHER COMPANIES

The Building Centre Group
www.buildingcentre.co.uk
Tel: 09065 161 136
Information for home improvers

The Construction Centre
www.theconstructioncentre.co.uk
Email: info@theconstructioncentre.co.uk
Tel: 01926 865825
Allows you to search through key categories such as general suppliers, professionals, tradesmen or contractors, local authority planning departments, construction industry, construction trade, full trade periodicals and news

The Rooflight Company
www.therooflightcompany.co.uk
Tel: 01993 833108
Company specializing in rooflights. Suitable for listed buildings and historical conversions

Index

Figures in italics refer to captions.

Index

Acknowledgements

The publisher would like to thank the following photographers, agencies and companies for their kind permission to reproduce the photographs in this book: 2 Simon Upton/The Interior Archive (Architect: Michael Trentham); 5 David Churchill (Architects: Architect Your Home); 9 Bob Smith/IPC Syndication; 10 Mark Luscombe-Whyte/IPC Syndication; 13 Jake Fitzjones/IPC Syndication; 14 James Balston/Arcblue; 19 Edmund Sumner/View (Architects: The Pike Practice); 27 David Churchill (Architects: De Metz Architects); 32–33 Pier Maulini/Vega Mg; 40 Nicholas Kane (Architect: Cany Ash & Robert Sakula); 45 Jan Baldwin/Narratives (Architect: Kay Hartmann); 46 Oliver de la Motte/Living Etc/IPC Syndication; 49 Courtesy of Keith Collie/Burd Haward Architects; 50 David Barker/Living Etc/IPC Syndication; 51 Paul Massey/Living Etc/IPC Syndication; 52 Chris Tubbs/Media 10 Images (Architect: Paterson Architects); 53 H. de Olmo/Cote Sud/Camera Press; 54 F. Amiand/Maison Francaise/Camera Press; 55 Luke White/The Interior Archive (Architect: Jonathan Clark Architects); 56 Jake Fitzjones/IPC Syndication; 58 Marianne Majerus (Garden designer: Jane Brockbank); 59 Luke White/The Interior Archive (Designer: Caroline Gardner); 60–61 David Giles/IPC Syndication; 62 Martine Hamilton Knight/Arcaid (Architect: Bauman Lyons); 65 above left Jake Fitzjones/IPC Syndication; 65 above right Tim Imrie/IPC Syndication; 65 below left Paul Tyagi/View (Architects: Studio MG); 65 below right Dominik Gigler (Architect: Jeremy Lim); 67 Chris Gascoigne/View (Architect: John Kerr Associates); 69 Jake Fitzjones/IPC Syndication; 71 Jan Baldwin/Narratives (Architect: Jonathan Clark); 72 Helen Fickling/Media 10 Images (Architect: Studio Azzurro); 74 Jan Baldwin/Narratives (London Penthouse of Darren Lock); 75 Liz Artindale/Narratives; 77 Andrew Wood/IPC Syndication; 78 Rachael Smith/Media 10 Images (Architect: Toby Falconer); 81 David Giles/IPC Syndication; 83 Courtesy of Spratley Architects; 84–85 Gaelle Le Boulicaut (Architect: Mark Guard; House of Rebecca Alleway, Set Designer); 86–87 Nick Cooney (Designer: Simon Pole, TILT Design); 88–89 Andreas Schmidt (Architects: Sanei Hopkins); 90 Edmund Sumner/View (Architect: PTP Architects Ltd); 92 Andreas von Einsiedel (Architect: Chris Pearson; Interior Designer: Joanne Pearson); 93 Gianni Basso/Vega Mg; 94 Simon McBride/Red Cover; 95 Jake Fitzjones/IPC Syndication; 97 Dominik Gigler (Architect: Jeremy Lim); 98–99 Giorgio Possenti/Vega Mg; 100 Andrew Paterson/Alamy; 103 Winfried Heinze/IPC Syndication; 105 above left Jake Fitzjones (Architects: Burd Haward); 105 above right Richard Powers (Designer Jakob Blom); 105 below left Darren Chung/Mainstreamimages/Architect: David Gregory; 105 below right Edmund Sumner/View (Architect: PTP Architects Ltd); 107 above Ray Main/Mainstreamimages/juerkearchitekt.en.de; 107 below M. Roobaert/Inside (www.wood-cottage-property.com); 108 Rachael Smith (Design: Pentagram Design); 109 Rachael Smith (Designer: Christian Foster); 110 Linda Vismara/Vega Mg; 111 Chris Tubbs/Media 10 Images (Owners & renovation: Paul and Karen Rennie); 112–113 Warren Smith/Red Cover; 114–115 Gianni Basso/Vega Mg; 116–117 Rachael Smith (Architect: William Tozer); 118–119 Kate Darby (Designers: David Connor and Kate Darby); 120 Ray Main/Mainstreamimages/Architect: Thorp.co.uk; 123 Ray Main/Mainstreamimages; 124 Tim Evan Cook/Red Cover; 125 Paul Tyagi/View (Pure Design & Architecture); 126–127 Ray Main/Mainstreamimages (concetto@centimetro.net); 129 Henry Wilson/Red Cover; 130 Lisa Cohen/IPC Syndication; 131 Edmund Sumner/View (Architects: The Pike Practice); 132 Nicholas Kane/Arcaid (Architects: Ash Sakula Architects); 133 Kilian O'Sullivan/View (Architects: Prewett Bizley Architects); 135 Ray Main/Mainstreamimages/Michaelis Boyd Ass Architects; 137 Jake Fitzjones/Living Etc/IPC Syndication; 138 Eugeni Pons (Architect: Anne Bugugnani); 139 Andreas von Einsiedel (Architect and Designer: Richard Weiss/3 S Architects); 140 and 141 above Jake Fitzjones (Architect: Stuart Forbes Associates); 141 below Ray Main/Mainstreamimages/Architect: Thorp.co.uk; 142–143 Jake Fitzjones (Architect: Paul Archer Design); 144 Jake Fitzjones/Living Etc/IPC Syndication; 146 Tham Nhu Tran/Living Etc/IPC Syndication; 147 Marcus Harpur (Designer: Christopher Masson, London); 148–149 Richard Powers/IPC Syndication; 151 Jake Fitzjones/Living Etc/IPC Syndication; 152–153 David Churchill (Architect: De Metz Architects); 154–155 Andreas von Einsiedel (Candy & Candy); 157 above M. Roobaert/Inside; 157 below Jefferson Smith/Media 10 Images (Architect: And Architects); 159 Edmund Sumner/View (Architects: The Pike Practice); 160–161 Sophie Munro/Red Cover; 163 Jerry Harpur (Designer: Luciano Giubbilei, London); 164–165 Tham Nhu Tran/Living Etc/IPC Syndication; 167 Robin Matthews/IPC Syndication; 168 Pier Maulini/Vega Mg; 169 Jake Fitzjones (Architect: Paul Archer Design); 171 Simon Upton/The Interior Archive (Owner John Dory/The English Stamp Co.); 172–173 Courtesy of Terry Pawson Architects; 175 Peter Cook/View (Architects: Woolf Architects); 176 Edmund Sumner/View (Architects: BACA Architects); 177 W. Waldron/Inside; 178 Courtesy of Ecospace; 179 Chris Tubbs/Media 10 Images (Architect: Sarah Wigglesworth); 180 Dominik Gigler; 182–183 James Balston/Red Cover (Architect: MPS); 184–185 Andrew Hayes Watkins/Media 10 Images (Interior Designer: Alistair Fleming, Fleming Associates); 186–187 Charlotte Wood (Architect: Jeremy King) **Every effort has been made to trace the copyright holders. We apologize in advance for any unintentional omissions and would be pleased to insert the appropriate acknowledgement in any subsequent edition.**

192